CLEAN SLATE

IMAGES FROM DOGEN'S GARDEN

Our greatest loss lies in failing to see
the natural things near at hand
and before our eyes.

—*Basho*

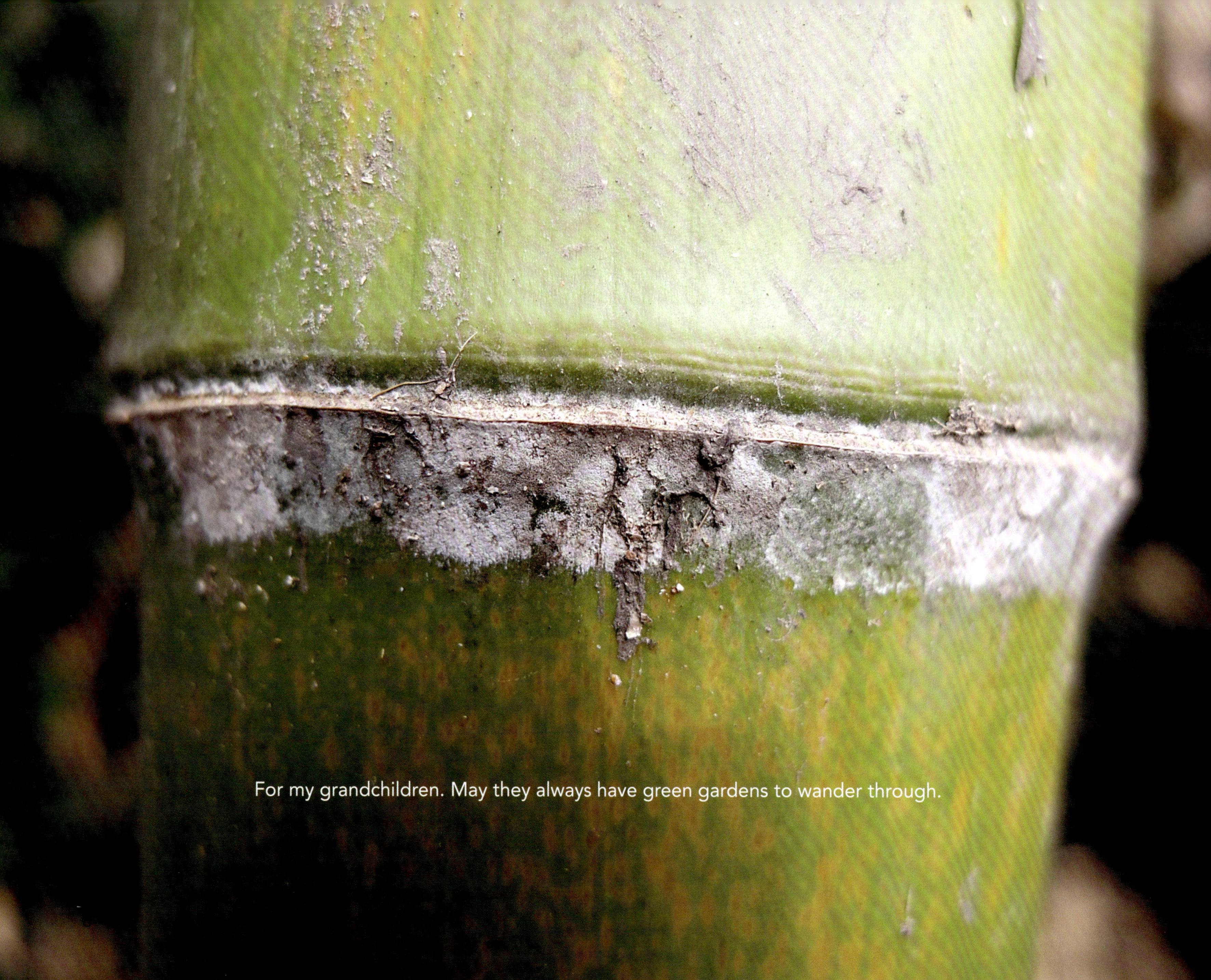

For my grandchildren. May they always have green gardens to wander through.

PREFACE

I wake up to gray clouds and the skyline of Kyoto. Outside in the street, I hear the murmurs of good morning. I gather my journal and camera to venture into Dogen's world. Why am I here? Who am I looking for? What am I looking for? In the hours and months of reading Dogen, he has become an acquaintance. His words prance about in my mind, making me giddy with their topsy-turvy grammar and hidden meanings. His ever-present references to nature bounce forward and link to my kinship with gardening. I like to think he sat in his *hojo* (the abbot's study) with paper in hand, his glance landing on a cherry blossom outside or an inspirational view from the *engawa* (the wooden platform that wraps around the building).

Looking and observing is a slightly different activity for someone studying Zen. It is more colorful than scientific scrutiny, more evocative than *hana kotoba*, the emotional words the Japanese use to define flowers. This is similar to but not the same emotional expression as in ikebana. For example, the *hana kotoba* of wisteria is "love and new life." As a Zen practitioner, I deeply consider and see the tentative, fleeting nature of a flower. I don't pick out the prettiest bloom I encounter, but see, without judgment, a flower browned at the edges, slumped with weather, eaten at the leaf's edge, yet still retaining a timeless beauty. The weathered bloom speaks to me; I listen, then observe, then take a photograph. Just there—that's it.

I follow Dogen's encouragement to hear not only with my ears but also with my eyes. Dogen, the teacher who brought Zen Buddhism to Japan from China, believed that nature was able to preach the dharma:

Just like the lotus
we too have the
ability to rise from the mud,
bloom out of the darkness and
radiate into the world.

In Zen, we honor all life as impermanent. The plant's condition as it exists teaches us about the present moment, to appreciate it like a bee diving into a blossom who finds it irresistible. She becomes one with the flower. Disappears into its essence. It's a living thing. Suzuki Roshi, the teacher who introduced Zen practice to America, cites the ancient text the Dhammapada, when Buddha said, "You should be like the bee collecting honey from flower to flower flying from flower to flower, without destroying the flower, without disturbing the beauty of the flower." When sharing this teaching, Suzuki Roshi added in his simple and profound English, "That is Buddhist way of helping people."

As the beekeeper at the San Francisco Zen Center, I see this every day. Our realization of nature is not dependent on names or categories or eons of time, but of actualization of *just there—that's it.*

Early on in my photographic work, I combined text and images. They leaned on each other to inform the viewer. The text or ideas came first, and then an image was conceived. In this spirit, I followed photographer Diane Arbus's idea board: the placement of a large, wall-sized chalkboard next to her bed. She scrawled numerous ideas, which germinated into projects. I did the same, just within reach of my outstretched arm. Here I filled my chalkboard wall with drawings, occurrences, and observations. Very much like visual dreaming, where objects were colliding with words, scribbles, images, feelings; explorations that were completely free and written without fear. I took it in the way Dogen suggested—not reading words in context but seeing words intuitively. A form of brainstorming without the brain. When the board completely filled, I erased it all with pleasure. All evidence, history, and ancestral markings gone. Pure emptiness.

I remembered that as a child, I delighted in using my slate board at school or at home. I loved wiping it off. Cleaning it. And beginning again. Years passed, and my love of nature emerged. In August 2011, at Green Gulch Farm (a Zen center in Marin County, California), I was reading Dogen and couldn't understand his text. I spoke with Abbot Steve Stuckey, who said, "Why don't you use your love of nature to understand Dogen? Your studies could be about the botany of Zen."

I worked in the gardens for many years and learned that weeding or removing plants cleared the soil—a kind of sweeping of my mind, tuning me in to how I was feeling that day. This led me to Japan. At Tofukū-ji temple gardens in Kyoto, I happened upon a striking event: a gardener wearing a blue denim apron. On his feet he wore traditional *jika-tabi* soft-soled boots, which allowed him to feel the ground without damaging it. He stood by a large chalkboard and an ancient tree waiting to be photographed. On the board in Japanese script I read the date, the tree's name, and the gardener's name below it. He had recently pruned the tree, and now his arms were crossed low in an X that resonated a gentle humility. More than a ceremony, this was a spiritual event to honor the ancestral tree and the gardener who cared for it. I was so stunned by this moment that I lost track of time and forgot all about my camera. It felt deeply intimate, as if I shouldn't even have been there.

The gardener erased the board. The stillness and the image of him and the chalkboard remained. Afterward, I reflected on Dogen's love of nature. I knew then that I wanted to photograph plants that Dogen encountered in the 13th century. I placed the blooms on the board to isolate the plant so that I could intuitively hear and see it. I then experienced the total exception of a single thing. By choosing one thing at a time, I could live in its thusness. John Ruskin, a 19th-century English art critic wrote:

> *The greatest thing a human soul ever does in this world is to see something, and tell what he saw in a plain way. To see clearly is poetry, prophecy, and religion—all in one. It is to be a seer.*

With my pictures completed, I returned to the writing of Dogen and invited five renowned Buddhist scholars to comment on the selections I had decided to include in this book. Dogen's ideas often are wrapped in nature, and these excerpts are particularly rich in those references. Each scholar was asked to pick from my selections and then contribute a response. The addendum includes these five contributions. I am extremely grateful for their time and thoughts. It is my intention that the addendum be a cross reference—a site to read and reflect, and then revisit the photographs. The knowledge these five scholars represent is far beyond my own capacity to reflect on Dogen with the written word.

There are few modalities to allow jumping back eight centuries to see what Dogen saw outside his window. Yet my camera made it possible. I invite you in. *Just there—that's it.*

MARCIA LIEBERMAN

INTRODUCTION

SEEING DOGEN'S WORLD BLOSSOM

This book is an invitation to imagine the world that Dogen saw, through Marcia Lieberman's photographs of the flowers and plants that surrounded Dogen in 13th-century Japan. Displaying these plants is an original, innovative approach to appreciating the world Dogen inhabited, and how this context informed his teaching.

In the addendum, five brief excerpts from Dogen's writings, with references to pine, rainfall, fish, chrysanthemum, peach, and plum, further illuminate his view of the natural world. Commentaries on these excerpts by five excellent contemporary teacher-practitioners in Dogen's lineage connect awareness of these elements with active awakening and expression.

In Dogen's Japanese language, there was no word, not even a concept, for "nature," as separate from or outside the human world. The Japanese *sansui*, literally "mountains and waters," denotes "landscape," but that whole field of the world is not separate from humans. Rather, people are merely a small part of the vast realm of what we might now call the natural world, appearing as tiny figures abiding amid the rocks and streams of East Asian landscape paintings.

Our relationship to this surrounding environment is a key theme in Dogen's teaching. In one of his earliest writing, *Bendōwa: Talk on Wholehearted Practice of the Way*, Dogen talks about the deep interconnectedness of practitioners and the world around, including "earth, grasses and trees, fences and walls, tiles and pebbles, and all things in every direction in the universe."

He says that all of these elements "carry out Buddha work, so everyone receives the benefit." This implies an impactful interaction, and he speaks of a mutual inconceivable guidance between humans and flowers. When each practitioner "displays the Buddha mudra with one's whole body and mind, sitting upright in this meditative awareness even for a short time, everything in the entire dharma world becomes Buddha mudra, and all space in the universe completely awakens." This space is no other than bamboo, plum, white chrysanthemum blossoms, red berries, gingko leaves, green weeds, and cedar branches.

In his book, *Sansui kyō: Mountains and Waters*, Dogen proclaims the liveliness of the landscape we occupy. Mountains are constantly walking. Not only are they constantly walking, but we can only truly learn our own walking by studying these mountains' walking. And of course the mountains are made up of its flowers and trees, as well as the rocks. Water is not merely flowing, but contains myriad worlds, each perceived differently by humans, fish, or dragons. In his essay, "Genjōkōan: Actualizing the Fundamental Point," Dogen describes how we see when out in the middle of a large body of water. An ocean or great lake seems round, with no end to the water, and none of the multitude of defining characteristics of a shoreline—no rocks, sands, trees, or docks—can be discerned. Similarly, when we look at a flower, what are all the multitudes of aspects of its true beauty beyond our vision? Even if we cannot know the full beauty of this world, still, Dogen says, our practice is fully involved with expressing this beauty.

The commentators of these photographs and the excerpts from Dogen further illuminate the intimate and dynamic interaction of practitioners and natural elements. Shinshu Roberts responds poetically to Dogen's poetry, proclaiming the immediacy of a fish leaping clear, or of a crane taking wing from its cold nest in the pines. Michael Wenger speaks of the tender wonder of deep connectedness, including Dogen's bond with our own flowering. Shohaku Okumura speaks of Dogen's love for plum blossoms, white amid the snow, and how all the particular flowers of the phenomenal world, even as they bloom and fade, can be informed by seeing the ultimate background of everlasting peace. Echoing Dogen, Reb Anderson encourages us to simply appreciate the images of green peach or plum trees as they appear, even as we sense their authentic, fresher green depths that Dogen's zazen reveals. Finally, Florence Caplow asserts that it is not enough to see Buddha in the flowery colors or hear Buddha in the raindrops and streams, but our practice is to cherish the earth fiercely. In our time when the natural order of each pine and flower is endangered, we have the responsibility and capacity to act as a member of our world to protect and sustain the natural forms of awakening.

Please use these images of flowers and leaves and Dogen's words that inspired to deepen and unfold the flower of your own caring and awareness.

TAIGEN DAN LEIGHTON

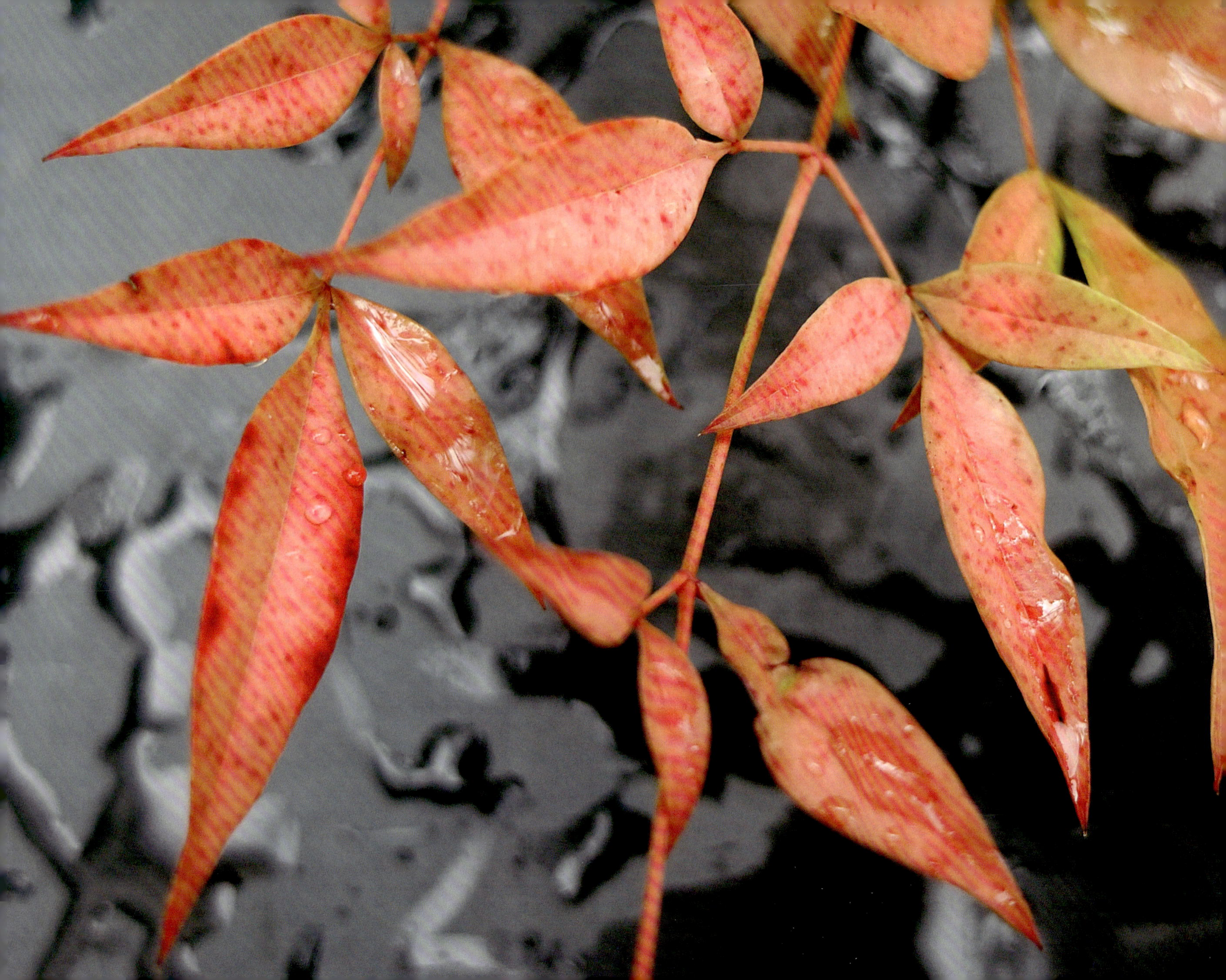

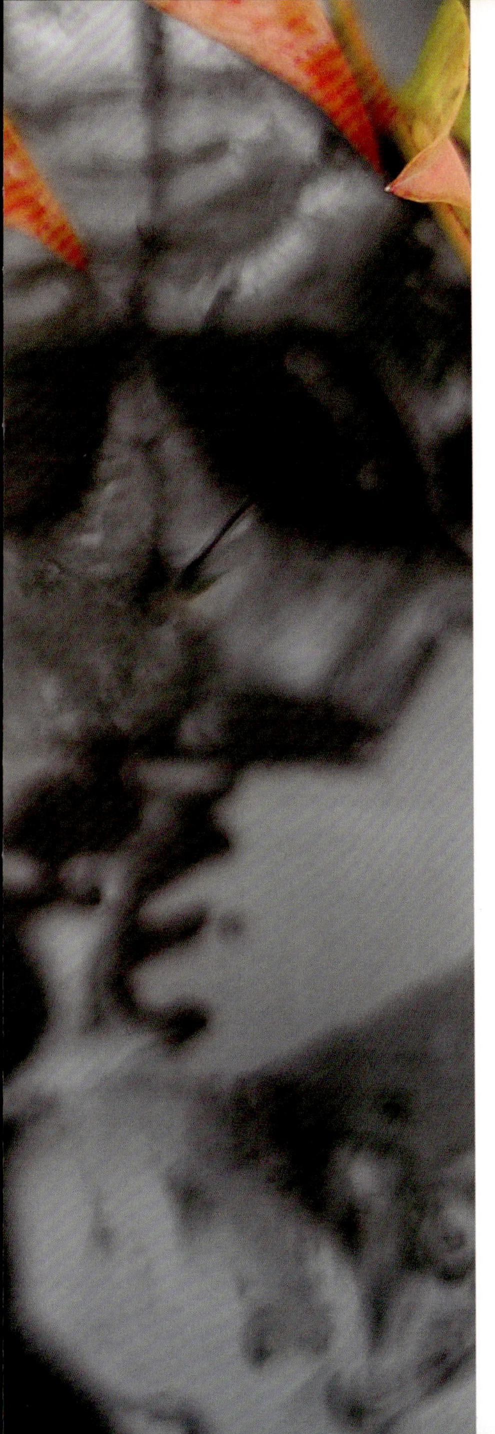

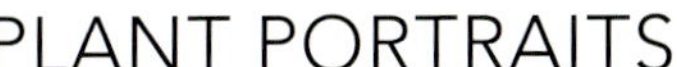

PLANT PORTRAITS

HYDRANGEA

HANA KOTOBA : Faith, heartfelt emotion, gratitude
JAPANESE : *Ajisai*
GROWING CONDITIONS : Shaded, moist soil.

While walking the perimeter of Mount Hiei in the mist and rain, I came upon this blossom. The hydrangea, or *ajisai*, shows itself in the rainiest of weather in Japan. The boldness and size of the bloom are tempered by the soft color and weather. It reached into my path with its head turned down. I had to lean over the stone wall barrier to reach it.

The bloom is past its prime. Is it really past its prime? Perhaps it is just a prologue for what is to come.

This atypical pink bloom resembles a beating heart and is particularly popular with florists. Story has it that an emperor gave hydrangeas to a maiden he loved as an apology for neglecting her when other business took up all his attention. For one's sweet tooth, candies made from the blossom are offered in spring. The leaves can be made into tea to bathe the statue of the Buddha on his birthday or to drink as a cleansing ritual.

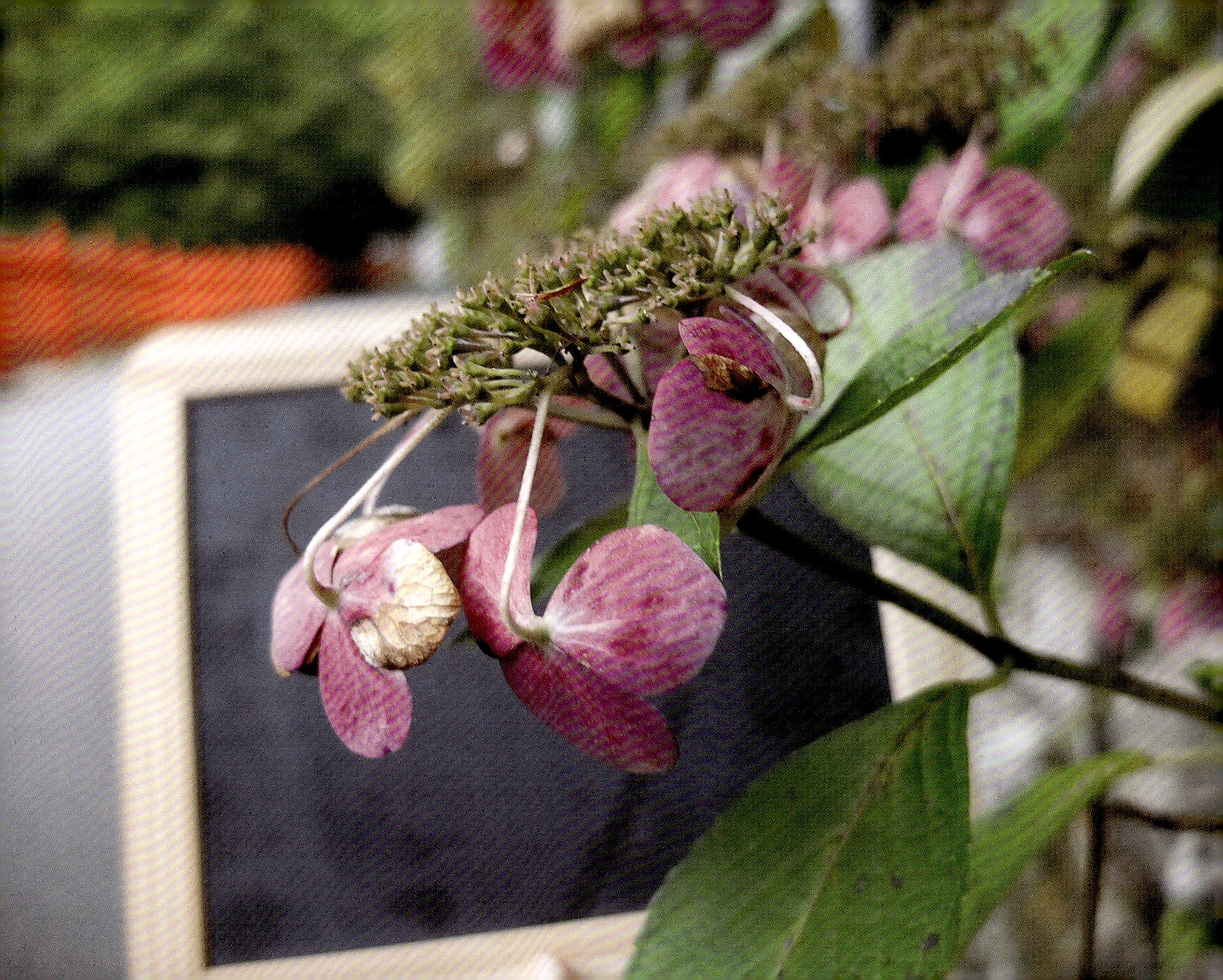

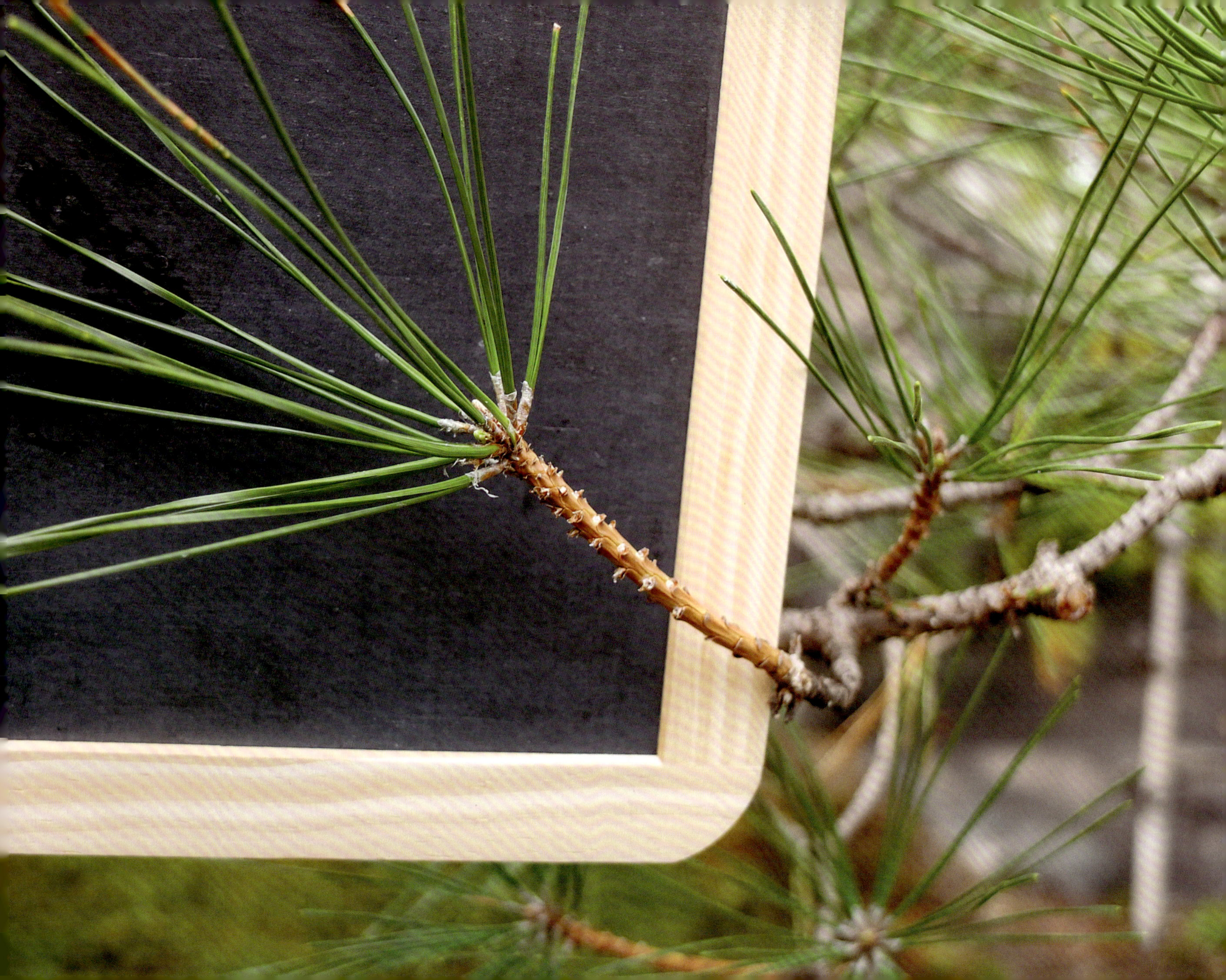

JAPANESE BLACK PINE

HANA KOTOBA : Happiness, long life, endurance, hope
JAPANESE : *Kuromatsu*
GROWING CONDITIONS : Full sun, well-drained soil, hardy, tolerates container.

There are many pines at Kennin-ji Temple in Kyoto. I stretched up to reach this branch and bring it near me. Only then did I see this branchlet stretching open like a fan.

Black pine is endangered in its native Japan from both pests and pollution. With unclean air the needles turn yellow and drop—an early indicator for us all.

Dogen loved these native plants and walked near them often. He said, "Pine and bamboo endlessly speak on my behalf."

Gardeners enjoy working with them and fondly say that the black pine takes to pruning like cloth to scissors—perhaps a metaphor for meditation.

Pine is part of the ikebana flower arrangement, "three friends of winter," along with flowering plum and bamboo. On festive occasions, you may enjoy this combination on an altar. It is pruned to suggest the effects of the wind.

Japanese history records the pine's presence: the famed wandering poet Basho passed by these pines on his journey along the *Narrow Road to the Deep North*; the fifth patriarch of Zen was said to be known as a pine-planting wayfarer; and Rikyu, a tea master, called the sound of water boiling in the teahouse, "the wind in the pines."

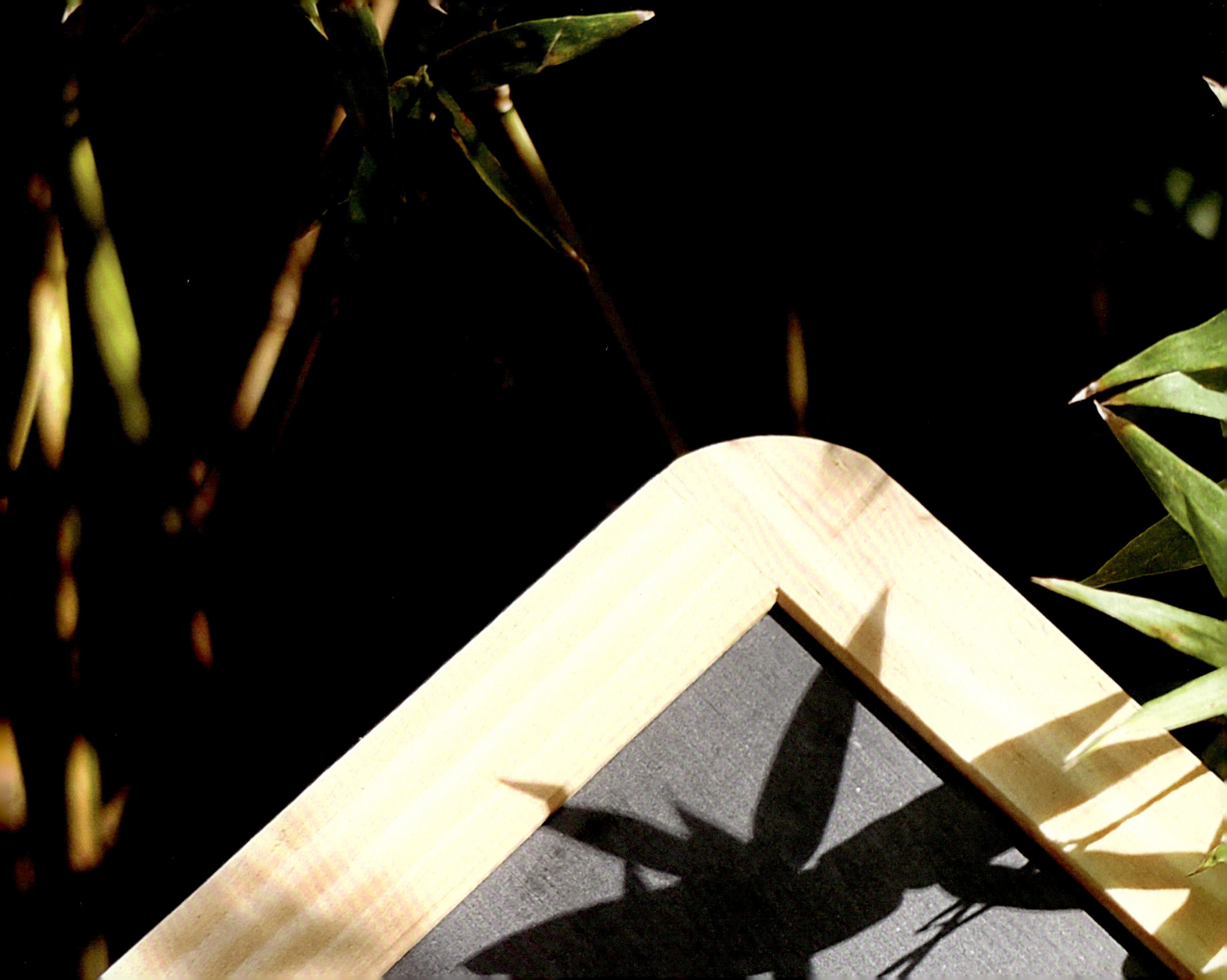

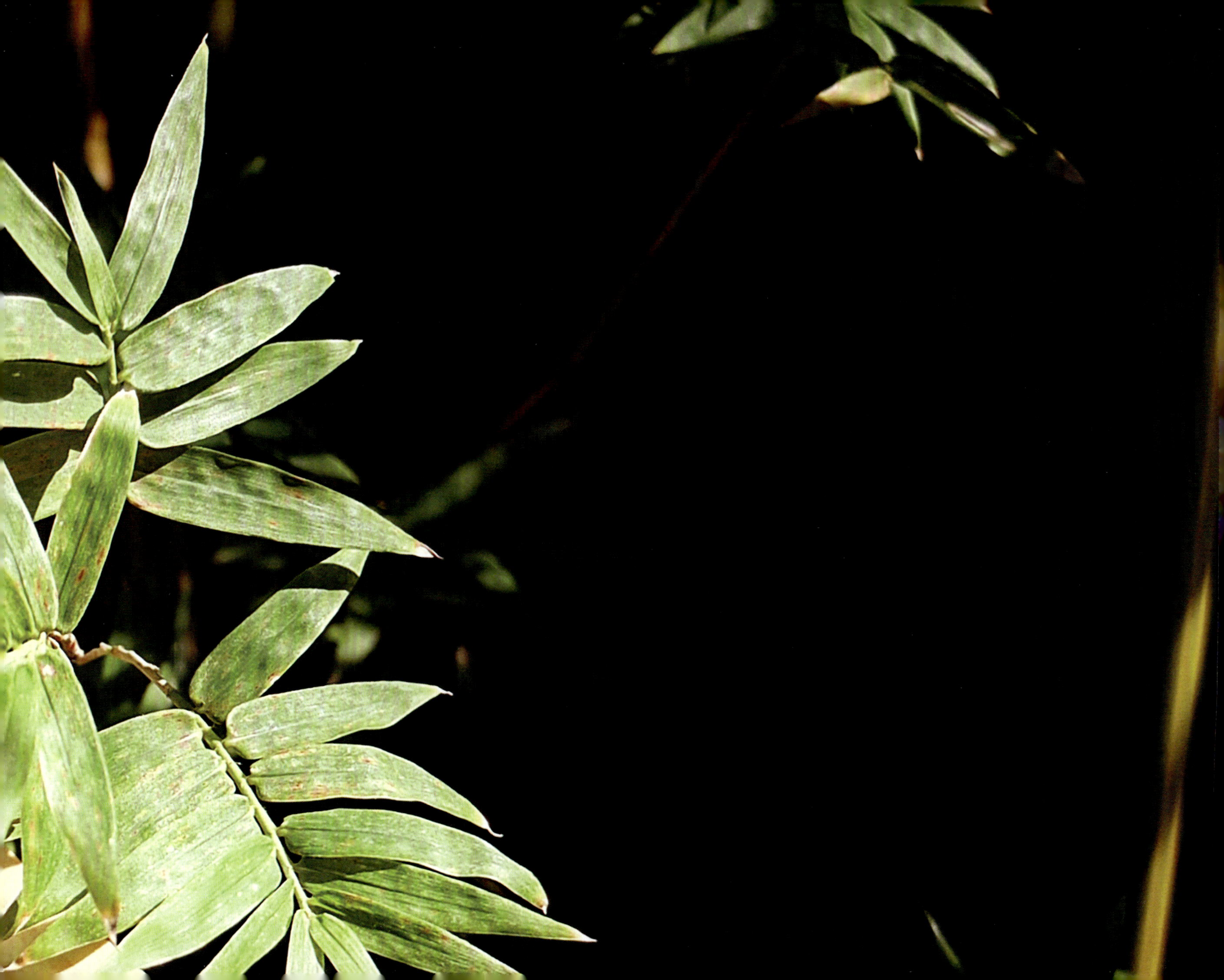

CAMELLIA

HANA KOTOBA : Love, pride, honor
JAPANESE : *Tsubaki*
GROWING CONDITIONS : Shady site. Keep roots cool by planting on north side of a building away from drying winds.

This bloom boldly facing me is a gentle pink, perhaps awaiting love.

I first met the camellia in an exquisite teahouse in Kyoto. The heavy full bloom spoke quietly in the dim room. Outside, gardeners walked around me in soft shoes trimming the hedges to a close perfection, the blooms dropping to the deep brown soil.

The color of the bloom is important. The meanings associated range from red (noble death/love) to yellow (longing) to white (waiting). How is it that love and death can both live in the same blossom? I imagine Dogen considering this duality with a camellia on his writing desk.

As this blossom falls to the ground, suddenly, it sounds like death—the beheading of an enemy soldier. When gift giving, avoid this bloom, since its specter is so profound.

A gentler cousin, however, grows on tea plantations near Kyoto and is harvested to make matcha tea.

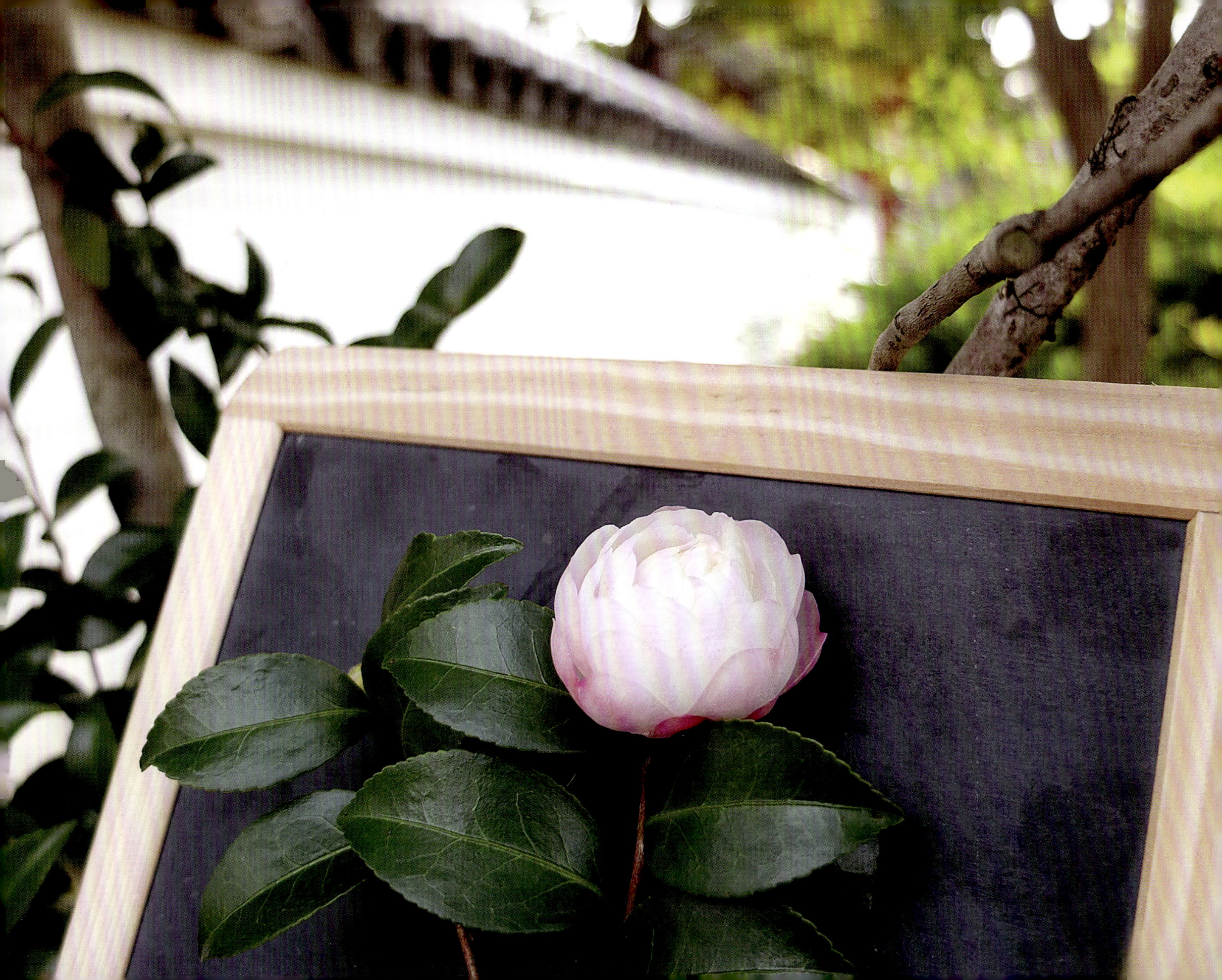

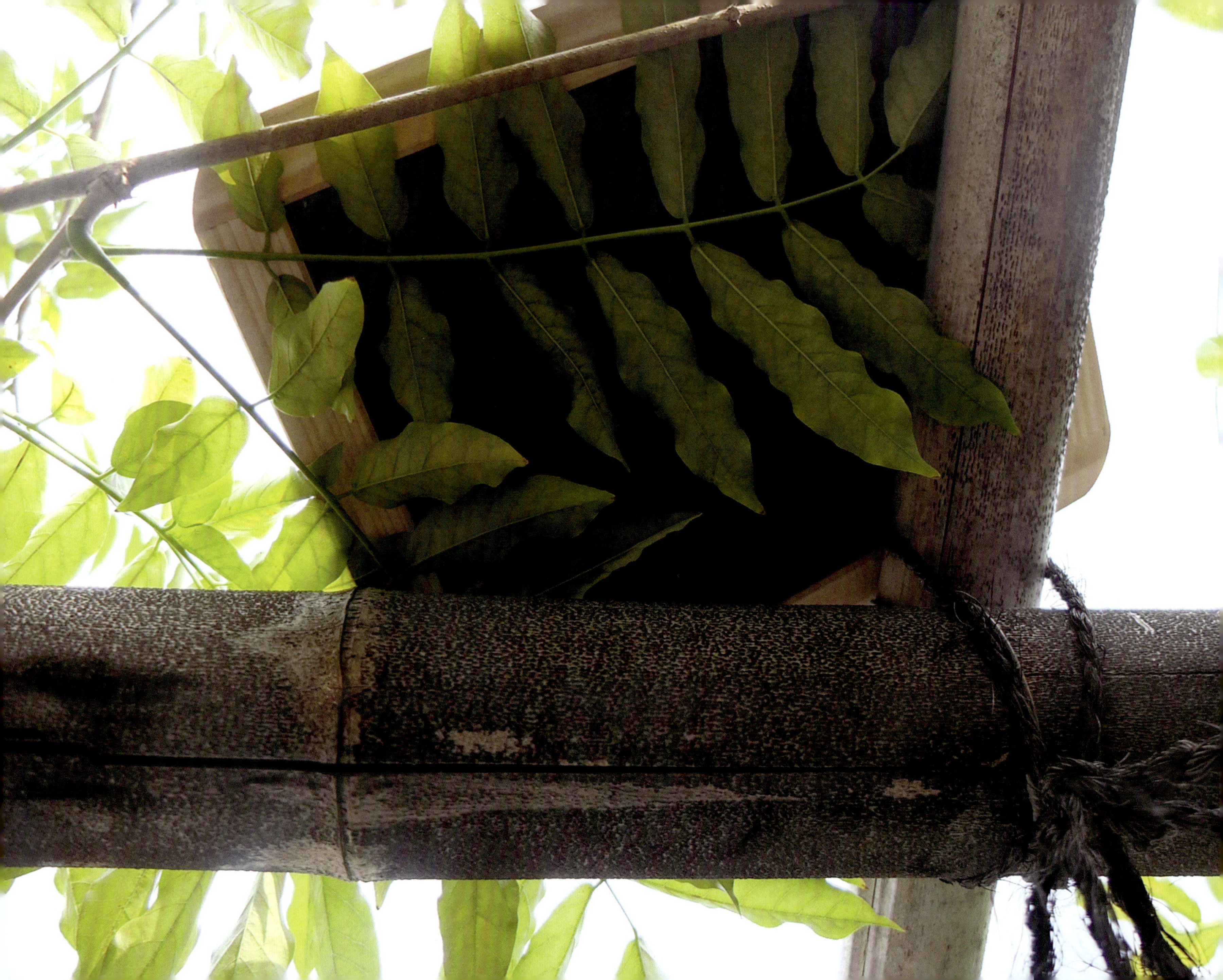

WISTERIA

HANA KOTOBA : Love, new life

JAPANESE : *Fuji masume*

GROWING CONDITIONS : Full sun with potassium- and phosphate-rich soil.

When I stood under this heavy bamboo trellis at Tenryū-ji Temple Garden in October, I felt how the wisteria vines had been carefully supported for years. It was autumn, so no blooms were present. I could see how its sinuous vines are sometimes harvested to make baskets.

The place where the new stems sprouted reminded me of footsteps in the zendo. Dogen wrote about twining vines in the Katto chapter of the Shōbōgenzō, perhaps outside his window.

Blooming in late spring, the blossoms lower their heads in gentle supplication, resembling a deep bow. The shape of the bloom is often represented on kimonos and in works of art. The flowers' deep purple color was forbidden to be worn by commoners and was relished by the nobility.

Near Rinso-in Temple, where I lived in Japan, the small town of Fujieda City strings yards of blossoms on all the street lamps and sells candy and snacks with a purple hue. For a month in spring, all the shops offer bundles of wisteria blossoms and deep-purple souvenirs.

JAPANESE CEDAR

HANA KOTOBA : Peaceful retreat
JAPANESE : *Sugi*
GROWING CONDITIONS : Deep soil, fast growing in youth.

Each morning after zazen at Rinso-in Temple in Japan, I would spend an hour sweeping the sugi branches that the night winds blew into the pristine courtyard. If I did not sweep them away, their sharp, sticky stems would root and nonchalantly turn this open space into a cedar grove. Their fury of color—a burnt orange hue—is like a stubborn sunset.

At Eihiji Temple, the sugi have tall, straight trunks that hold up the bell tower. The name sugi means "hidden parts," but they are the most present evergreen tree in Japan. This national tree reaches incredible ages—some over 7,200 years old in Yakushima. The upright posture of these trees surely must have inspired Dogen.

In the 16th century, a feudal lord named Matsudaira Masatsuna was too poor to donate a stone lantern at the funeral of the shogun Tokugawa Ieyasu. He requested instead to be allowed to plant an avenue of sugi, so that "future visitors might be protected from the heat of the sun." Over 22 miles long, the Cedar Avenue of Nikkō still exists.

The sugi is also known for its architectural effect of shou sugi ban, preserving wood, which requires charring the house to a jet black color impervious to weather and pests. At the teahouse at Green Gulch Farm in California, I carefully used a blowtorch on the upright beams of the garden fence. I had to pay constant and complete attention to create the effect.

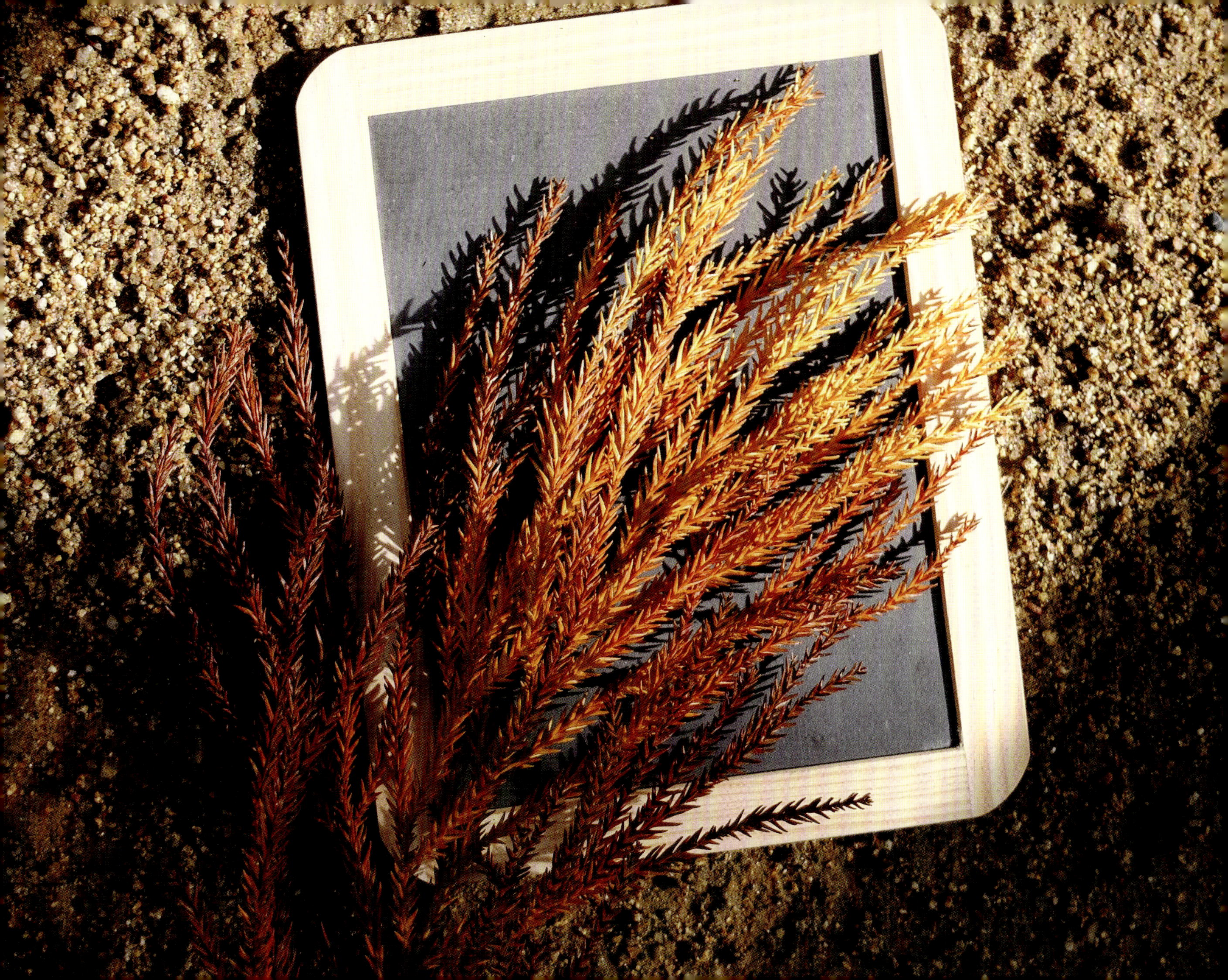

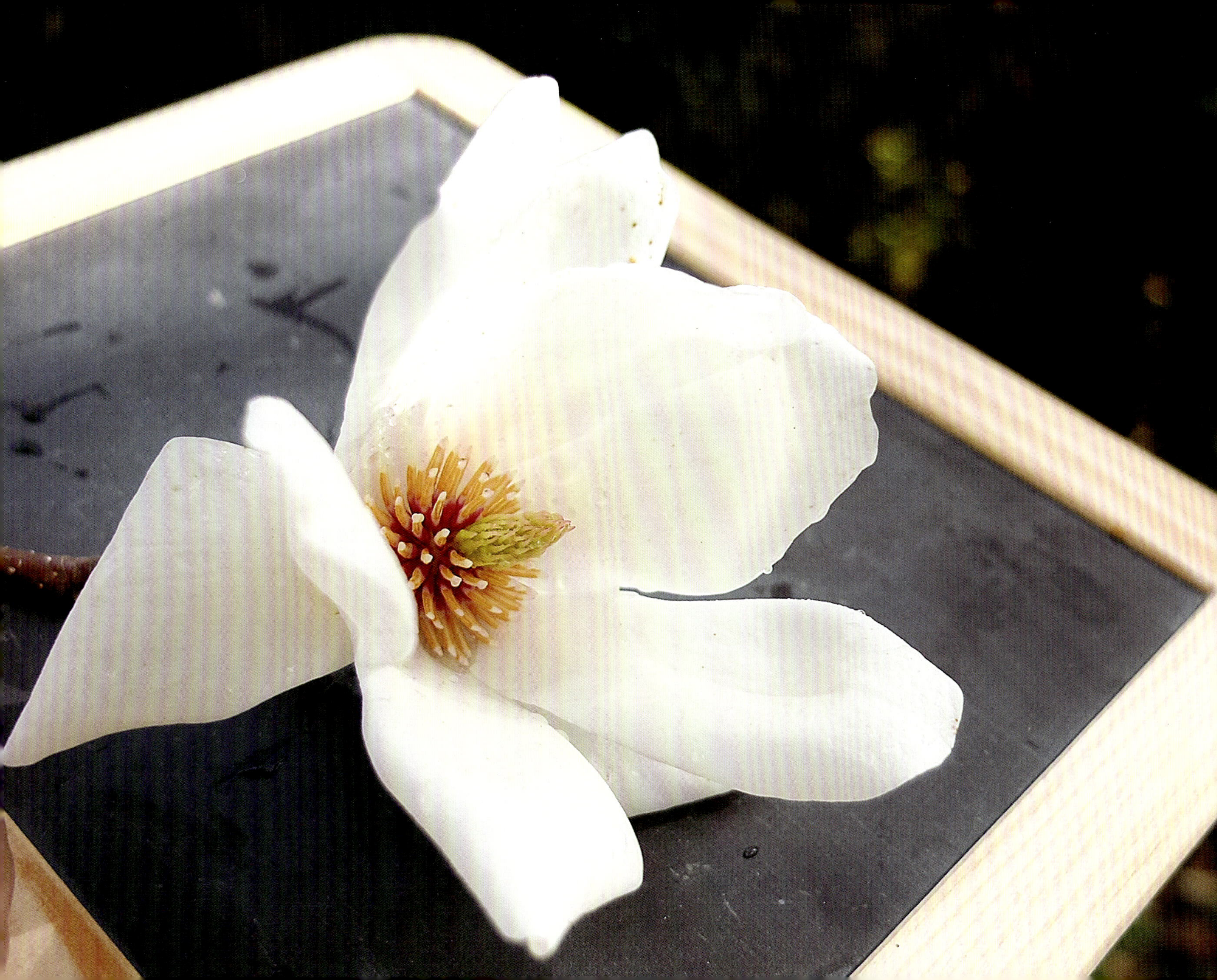

MAGNOLIA

HANA KOTOBA : Natural, sublime, love of nature
JAPANESE : *Haku mokuren*
GROWING CONDITIONS : Slightly acidic moist soil with some sun.

This is an ancient plant. While pushing my nose deeply into the bloom, I found a slight delicate fragrance. The tall tree I stood under resembled a giant flower arrangement. This tree is unique in that the bloom arrives first on the bare branches.

The center carpel of the bloom entices me in just like it does the beetle, a frequent visitor that meets it face-to-face.

The Chinese first cultivated the magnolia in 600 CE and used it as a symbol of purity in the gardens of the emperor's palace. Because of the bloom's durability and association with invigorating a person's chi, they are often given on the occasion of birth. The leaves on these trees, which can grow for 120 years, are used in the kitchen and the bark for medicinal healing. The petals I took home to flavor my rice.

LOTUS

HANA KOTOBA : Far from the one he loves
JAPANESE : *Hasu*
GROWING CONDITIONS : Muddy soil with at least three feet of water. Seeds can wait 200 years to germinate.

Crossing the long bridge at Tenryū-ji in Kyoto, I noticed lotus plants along either side of my footsteps. They were falling, bending, drifting in the shallow dark water. Here and there a fish or frog broke the surface. The shallow gray mimicked my slate board.

This plant is a popular Buddhist symbol of spiritual awakening. Rooted in the mud, it stretches long until the blossom energetically rises up to the sky. It is the flowering that is most important and can only be imagined in this image. Next season? Yet the sturdy leaves caught my attention, and I remembered that warriors prefer the foliage, which connotes a virile spirit.

In this ancient garden, designed by Musō Soseki to blend zazen and gardening, the pond is a symbol of the sea. Here the lotus makes a cracking sound when it opens.

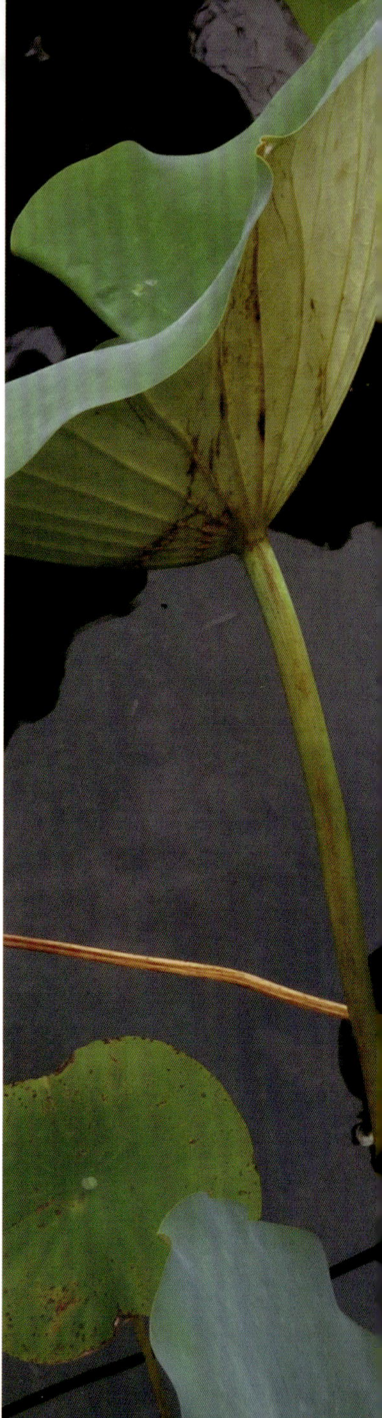

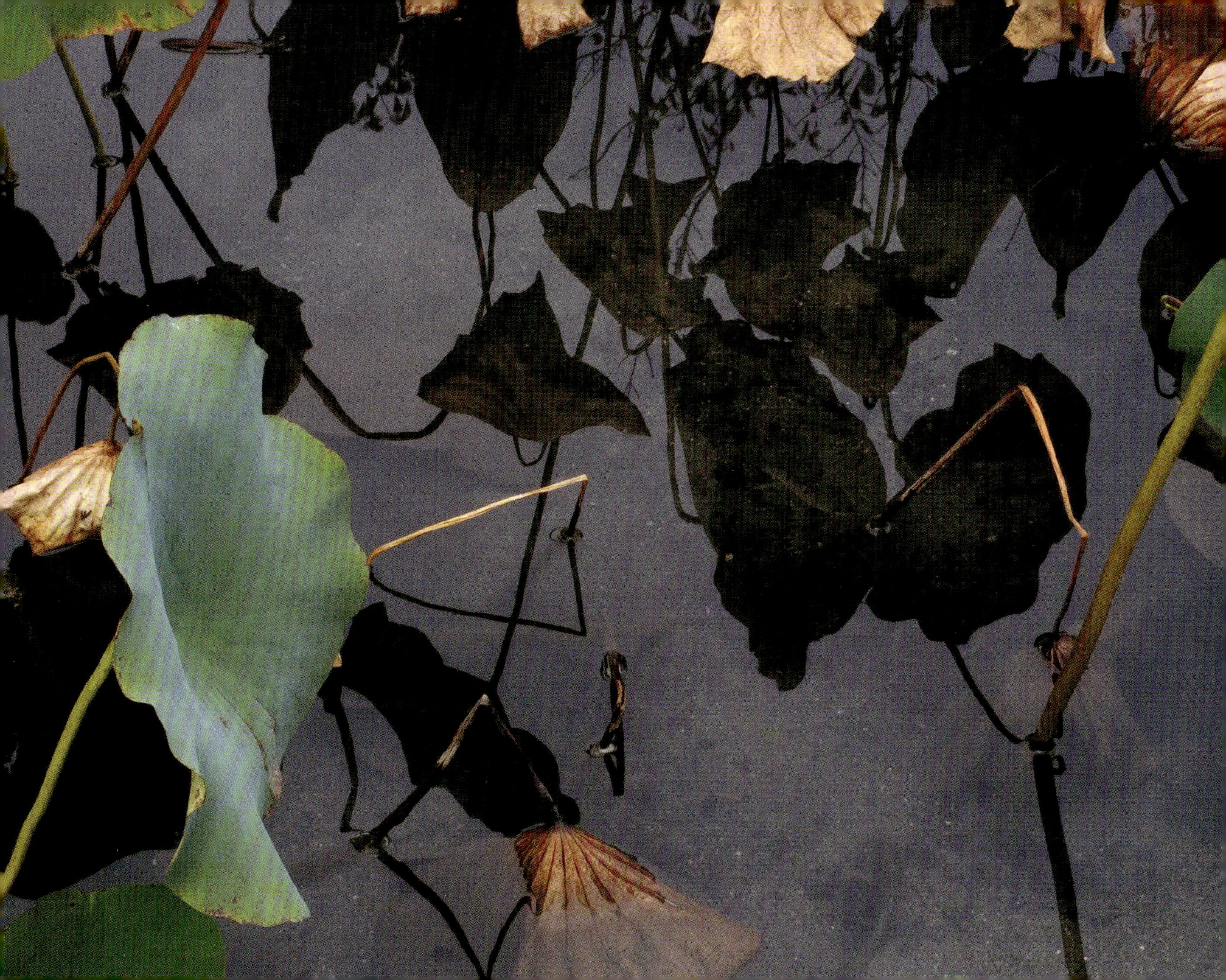

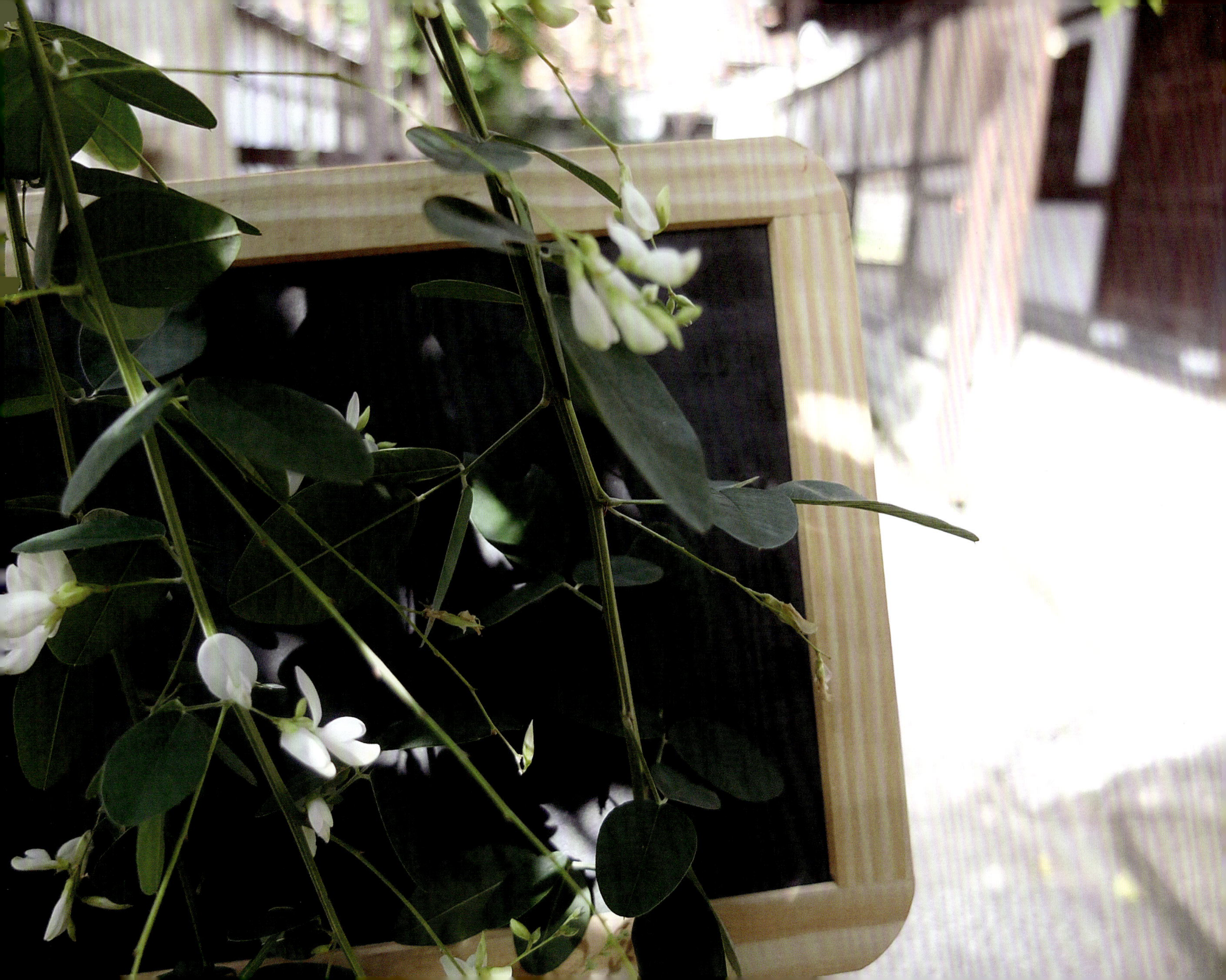

WHITE PEA

HANA KOTOBA : Departure, delicate pleasure, tender memory
JAPANESE : *Suitopi*
GROWING CONDITIONS : Moist soil, sun, a trellis to climb.

I had to duck to get past this large vining plant. There were small miniature peas tucked into the foliage like little secret pearls. At Kennin-ji Temple, this ancient native plant continues to grow as if to proclaim its longevity. It is one of the oldest plants on earth, and fossil records have been discovered.

In the teahouse, I sometimes use one long singular branch for the *chabana* arrangement in the tokonoma. *Chabana* is the specific flower display for the Japanese tea ceremony. Though it is fundamentally a form of ikebana, it comprises a genre unto its own.

The white pea is notable for its short life: barely surviving a few hours in a vase.

In the field, the pea is grown as a vegetable, but this particular species is delicate and would hardly provide much sustenance.

JAPANESE MAPLE

HANA KOTOBA : Neatness
JAPANESE : *Momiji, iroha-kaede*
GROWING CONDITIONS : Steady supply of water through root zone, filtered shade.

In winter, when a chill breeze whisks off the maple leaves from their branches, the Japanese exclaim, "It's *kogarashi*!" or "wintry wind." I arrive at the Saiho-ji temple garden in Kyoto after *kogarashi* when the deep red leaves of the maple are vibrantly carpeting the ground. A dedicated pruner works on these maples nearby. I notice his timing and attention to detail and how essential it is for the tree's healthy growth. I learn my first lessons in pruning a maple.

This garden, known for its lush moss in stark contrast to the deep red hues, touches me, and I pick up a few leaves to later tuck into books like little secrets. The foliage of the maple is so exquisite that starting in the seventh century, it was used solely for a bouquet. The branches and leaves are used as a treatment in traditional Chinese medicine.

In Buddhist practice we make mudras with our hands in forms that are ancient. This leaf looks like a mudra in the garden—palm open and calmly looking up. In fact, the Japanese names for this tree—*kaede and momiji*—are references to hands of frogs and babies, respectively.

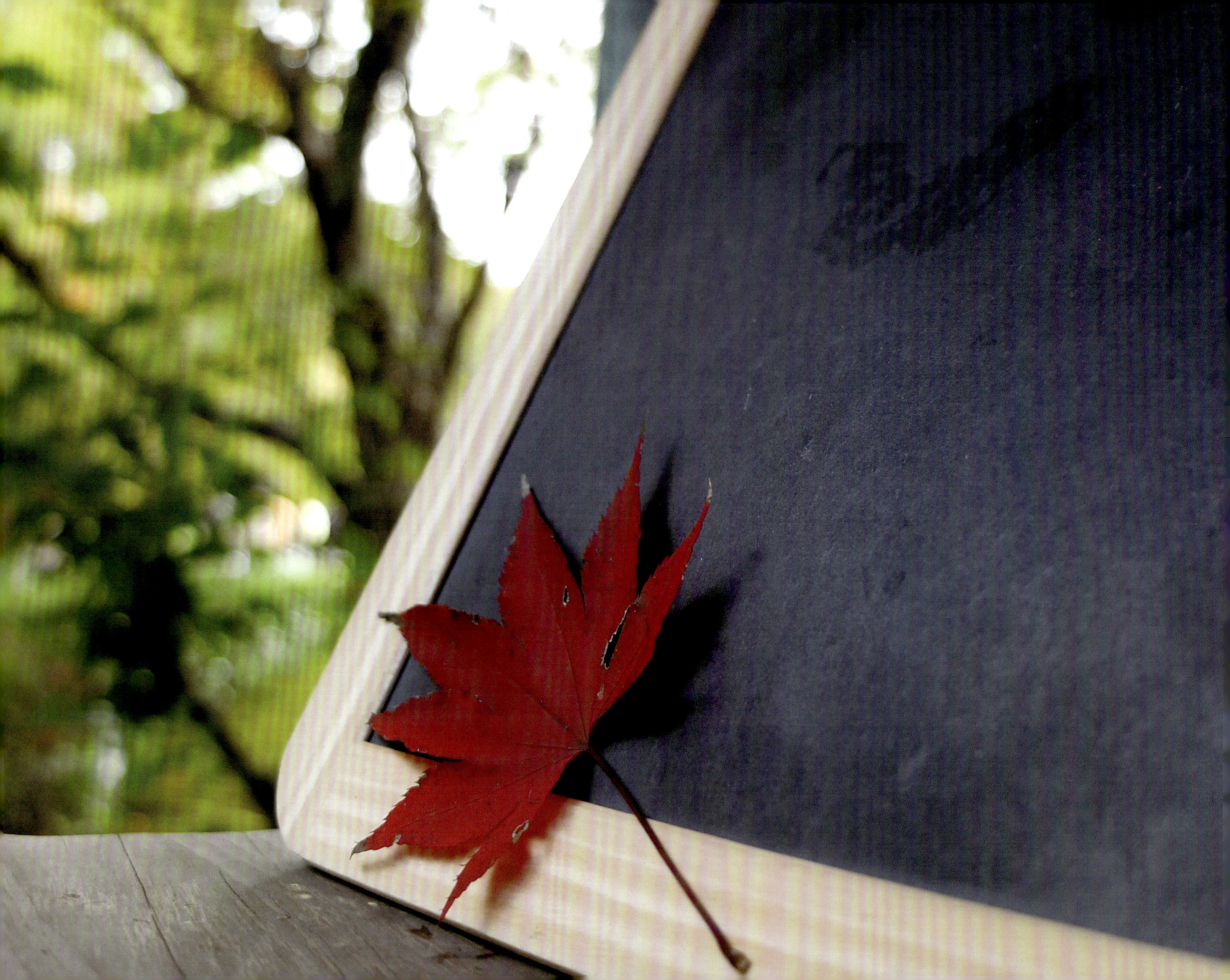

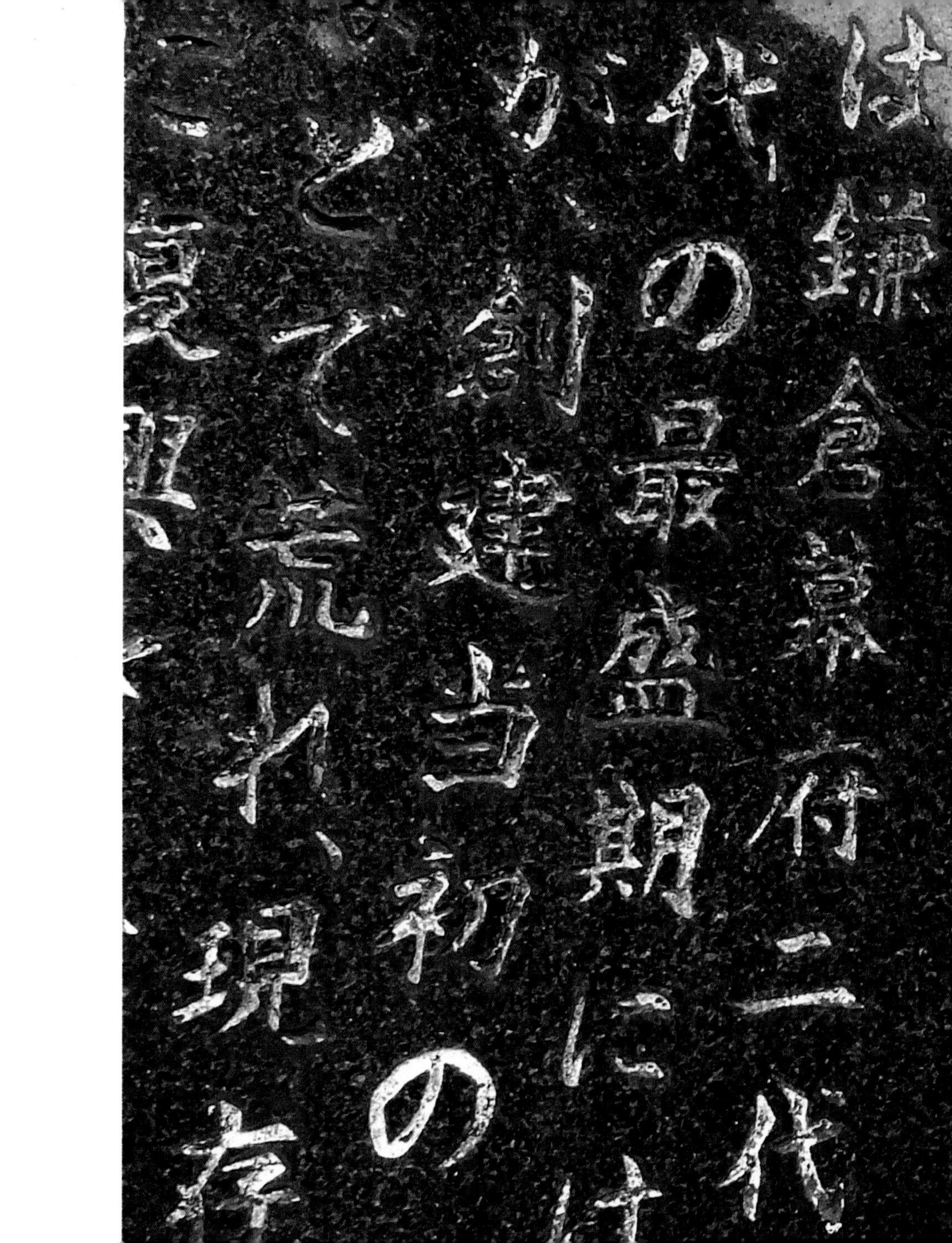
は鎌倉幕府二代
代の最盛期に
が、創建当初の
荒れ、現存

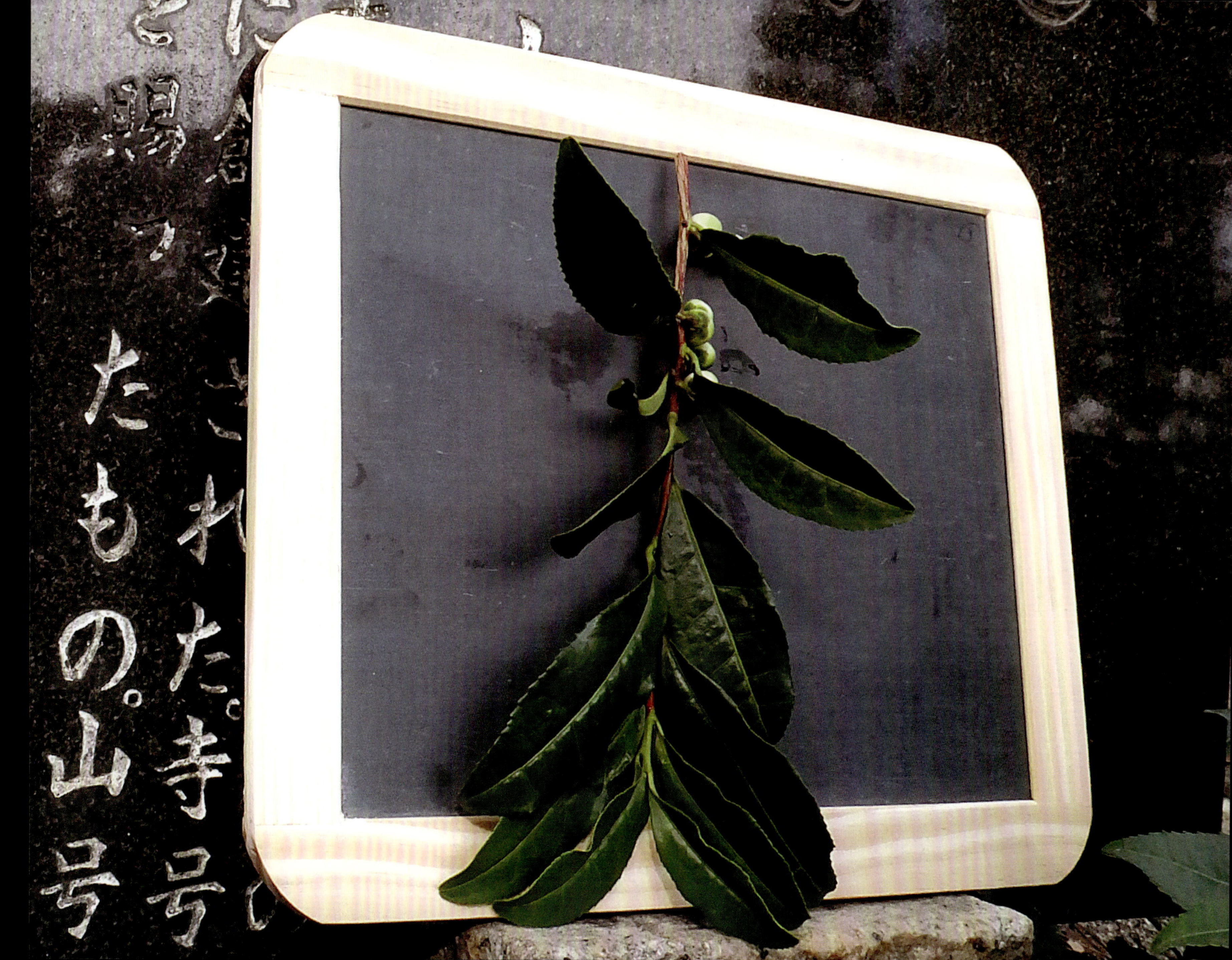

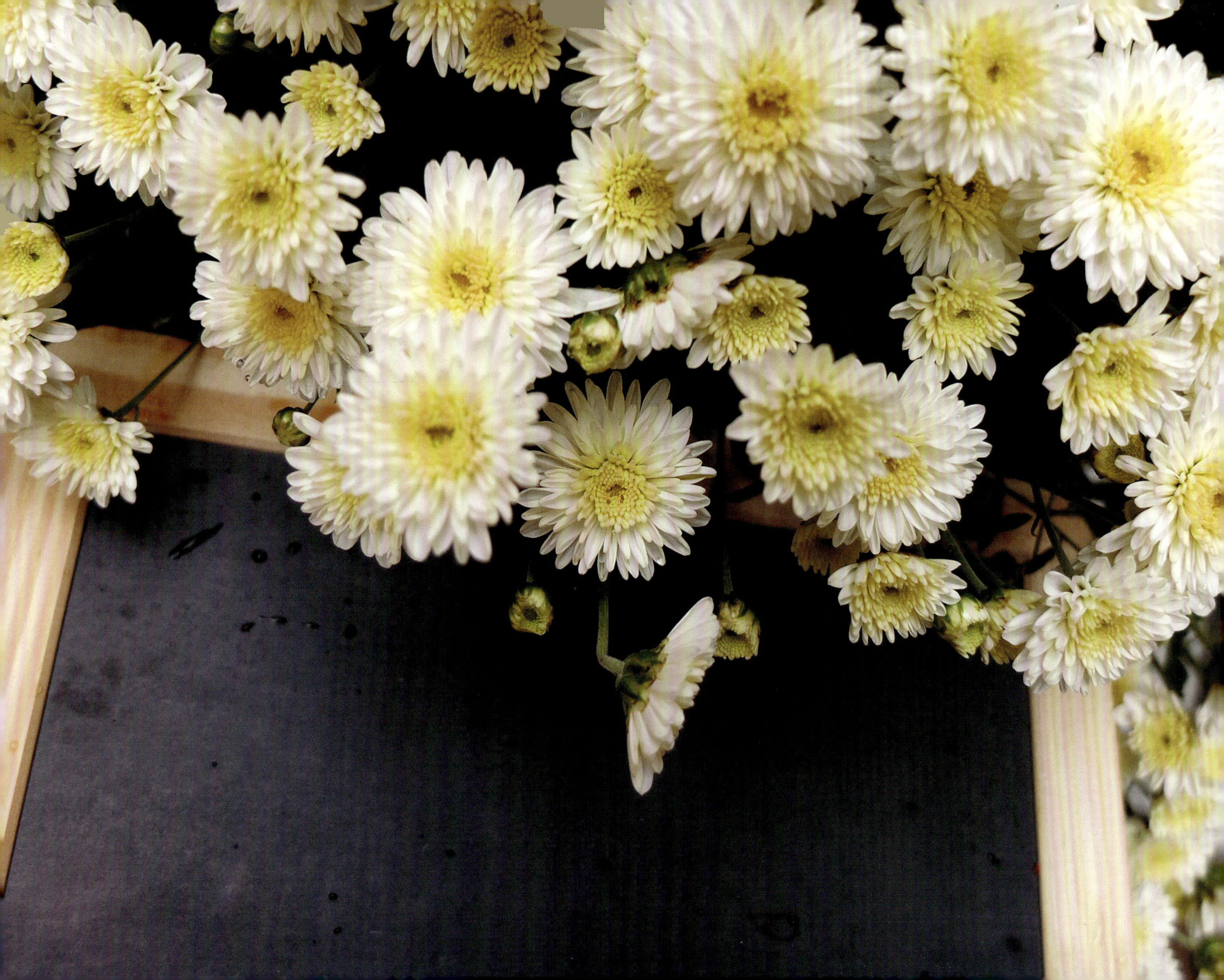

YELLOW CHRYSANTHEMUM

HANA KOTOBA : Vague memories, noble simplicity
JAPANESE : *Kika*
GROWING CONDITIONS : Full sun, light soil, may freeze in cold winter.

Walking in the city, I discovered that no matter how small a front yard may be, there are plants and blooms crowded near each door. How happy I am to see these clusters, gathered together like good friends, inviting me in to join their communities.

Autumnal days give these blooms time to grow, and they emit a slight sweet fragrance when touched. Each day their brightness shifts, and the shapes of old blooms bend toward the earth.

Originally grown as a flowering herb in the Nara and Heian periods, the plant was used for heart disease and colds. Their petals make a popular tea for warm weather too. Because the leaves are edible, they can be used in salads, vegetables, and hot soup, and as a sashimi garnish.

Chrysanthemum plants have even been shown to reduce indoor air pollution.

JAPANESE HAWTHORN

HANA KOTOBA : Waiting for success
JAPANESE : *Shirinbai*
GROWING CONDITIONS : Full sun, light shade, slow growing, thrives in thickets near seashore.

Sometimes this plant is referred to as yeddo, which was the former name of Tokyo. When I was taking my morning stroll at the Kyoto Botanical Garden, the vigorous green color of the hawthorn leaves stood out like an actor upstaging her cast. Other plants around it faded passively with the season, but the hawthorn defied time, as if it were eternal spring or summer.

It is one of the most common native plants used in gardens, and the blossoms emit a honey scent.

The fruits resemble small figs and are used in the 400-year-old tradition of dyeing pongo silk. Also, when cooking fish, the berries are added to the broth to soften the bones and make them edible.

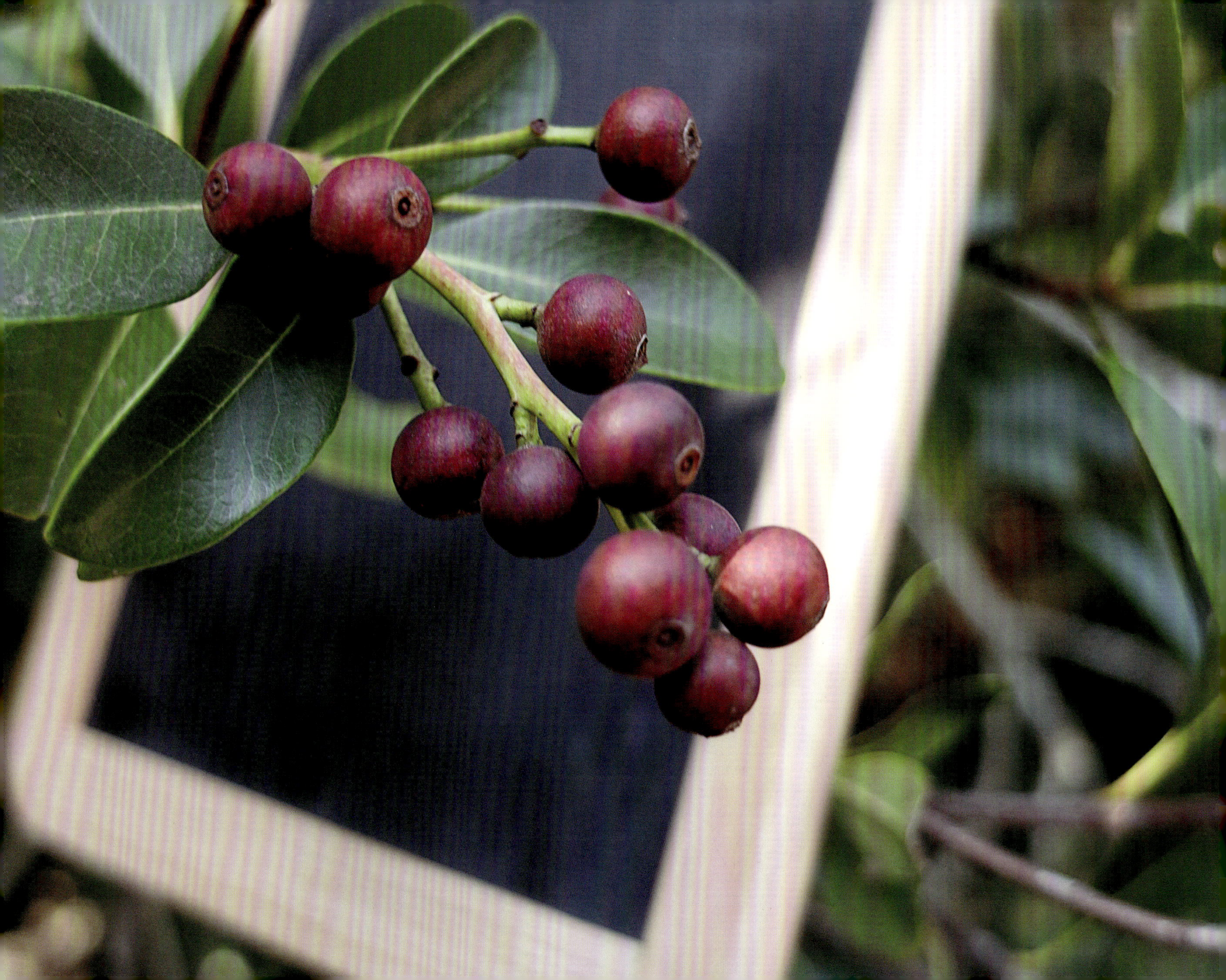

BAMBOO

HANA KOTOBA : Moderation, pliancy, constancy, abundance, pure innocence
JAPANESE : *Take hachiku*
GROWING CONDITIONS : Abundant watering.

As I rode a train in Japan, something magical caught my eye: the rolling hills seemed to sway and shimmer in the wind. The Arishiyama Bamboo Grove and its tall shoots also clinked together, sounding like a small orchestra of percussive, like-minded instruments.

This plant has so many esthetic charms: the swollen nodes like joints on a limb; the peeling outer layer when the grass reaches a certain size. It is called "the prince," being the most primitive of grasses.

Buddhist practice is slow and quiet, in stark contrast with the bamboo, which can grow several feet a day. How can it be a favored symbol of moderation—perhaps because of its enduring and prolific patience? Most temples I visited had a grove of bamboo as part of a sacred barrier against evil.

The pliancy and moderation meanings ascribed to bamboo are inspired by the knots that separate segments. Like small apartments in a building, these units tie together for sturdiness, but because they are separate, the bamboo can bend. Perhaps moderation is the middle way.

Bamboo has numerous uses. Here are just a few: food source, fabric, building material (it rivals steel in compressive strength), decorative element in houses, chopsticks, charcoal, flooring, asymmetrical archery bows called *yumi*, everyday utensils, New-Year altar arrangements. All these uses have been established since the Late Jōmon Period, 2000 BCE.

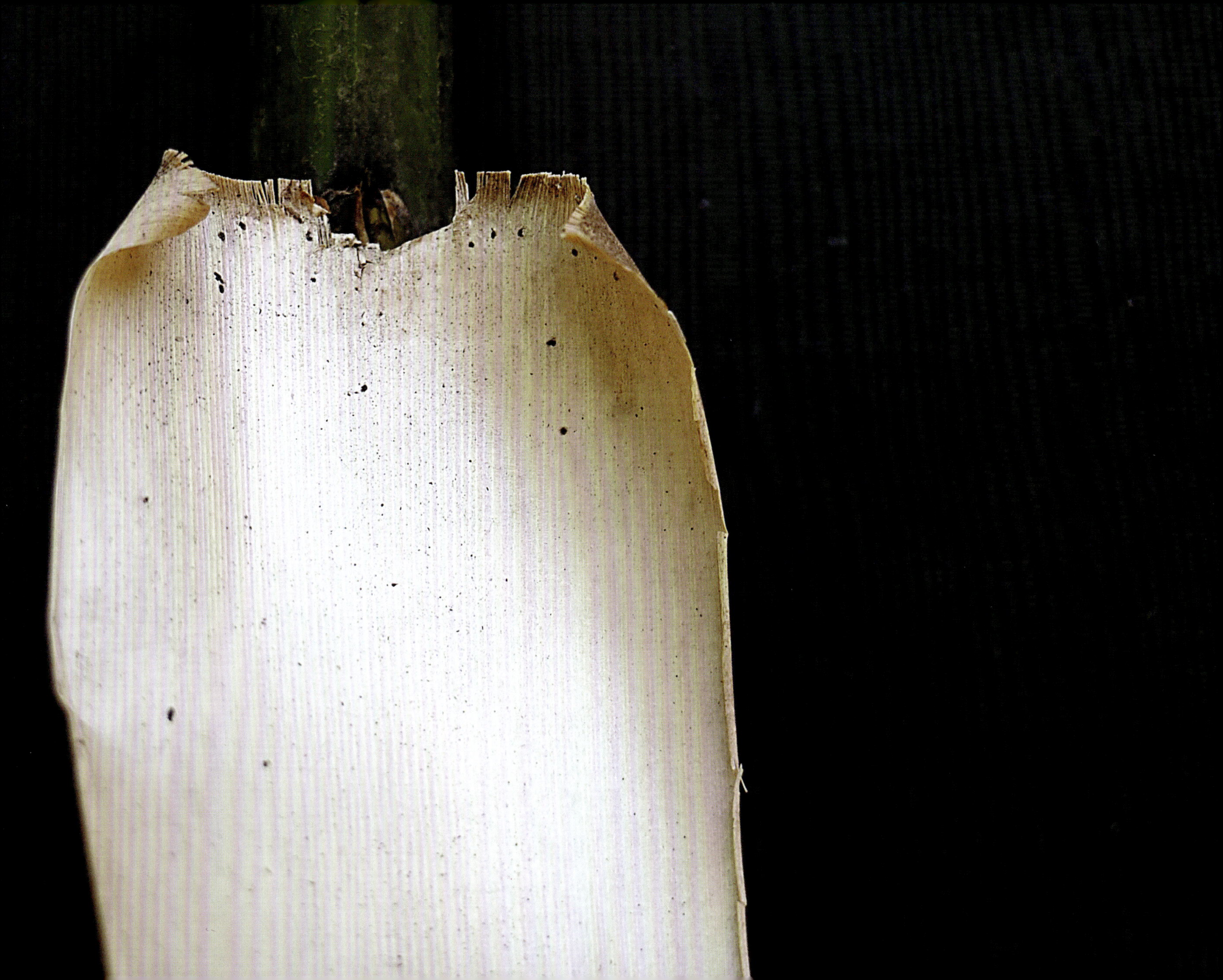

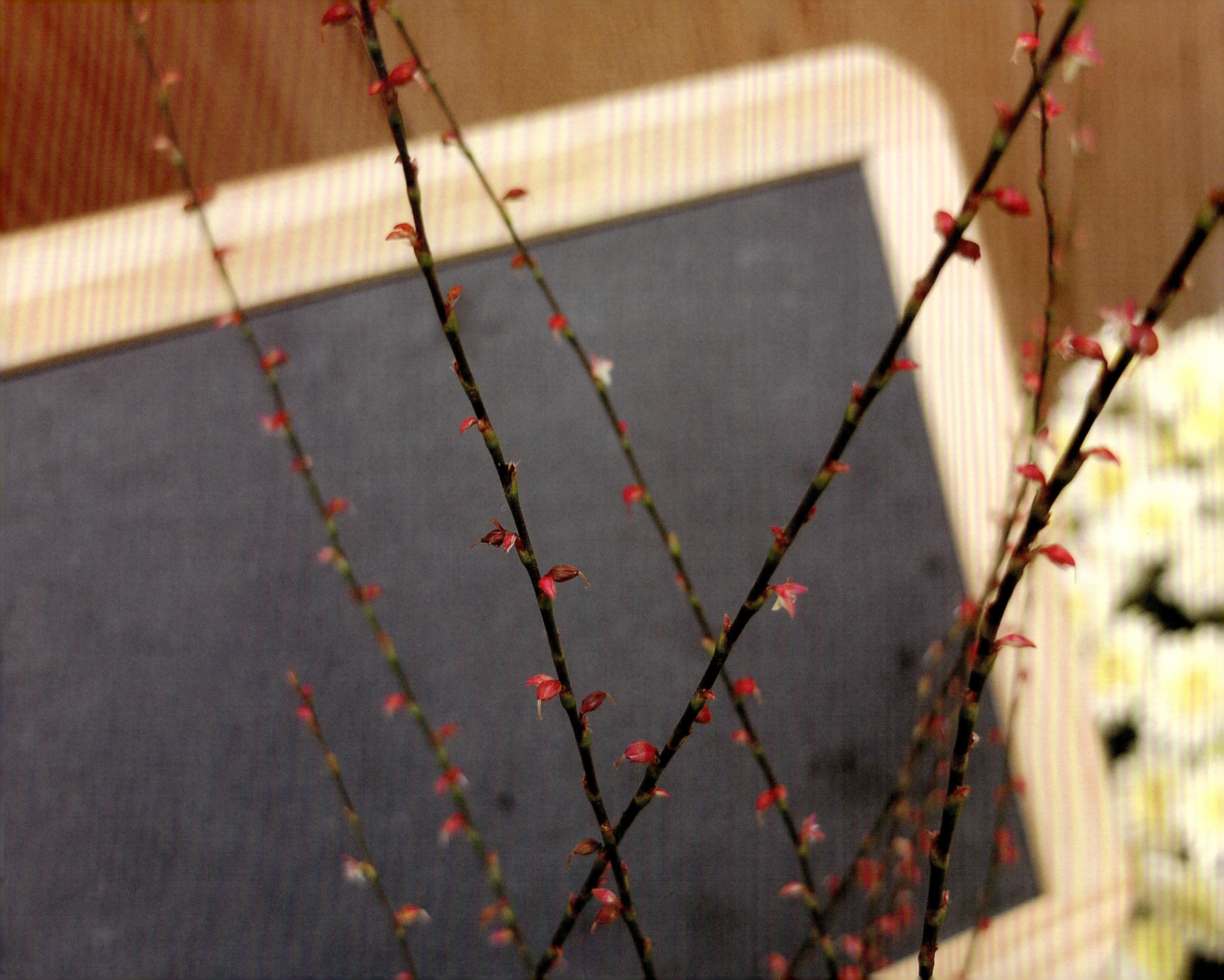

JAPANESE KNOTWEED

HANA KOTOBA : None
JAPANESE : *Mizuhiki*
GROWING CONDITIONS : Sun, humus-rich soil.

This plant has long, thin branches with miniature red and white blossoms. The Japanese love this bloom so much that they make a copy of it out of twisted rice paper. When you receive an auspicious gift, the red and white cord is wrapped around it and fastened with a knot. This ancient Japanese art form took me several years to learn before I could make a knot on the stem of a ceremonial pine branch.

Here we see something sculptural with jointed stem and myriad blooms. Its heart-shaped leaves fade within minutes of clipping the stalk.

The knotweed reminds me that in Buddhism "the endless knot" symbolizes samsara, the endless cycle of birth and death, the twining of wisdom and compassion. Since the knot has no beginning or end, it also symbolizes the wisdom of the Buddha.

Dogen, encouraged by this saying, wrote, "Sit near a bright window and reflect on this, on mellow and flower-filled days. Sit in a plain building and remember it on a solitary rainy evening."

Japanese knotweed is occasionally eaten.

TREE PEONY

HANA KOTOBA : Good fortune, compassion, noble spirit
JAPANESE : *Botan*
GROWING CONDITIONS : Drought tolerant; five to six hours of sun daily and moist forest clearings.

The bud of this powered-up peony at Uji was about to burst into a 10-inch bloom shouting, "Spring has arrived!" I can see why it's said that the peony looks like the unkempt mane of a lion, since its profusion of petals appears as shaggy as an animal's coat. Perhaps this lion inference began in the sixth century with Shakyamuni Buddha being a member of the Shakya (lion) clan.

Furthermore, it's thought that Buddhist monks were responsible for transporting the tree peony from China to Japan in the eighth century. Another story credits Kukai, the famous Buddhist scholar of esoteric Buddhism, for introducing the tree peony. It's not a coincidence that after his death he was called Kobo-Daishi, the grand master who propagated Buddhist teaching. Surely with the same enthusiasm he propagated the peony in his garden.

The petals can be lightly boiled and used for a tea-time delicacy. Historically, the plant was not seen as an ornamental but rather as an important medicinal plant for treating ailments like coughs.

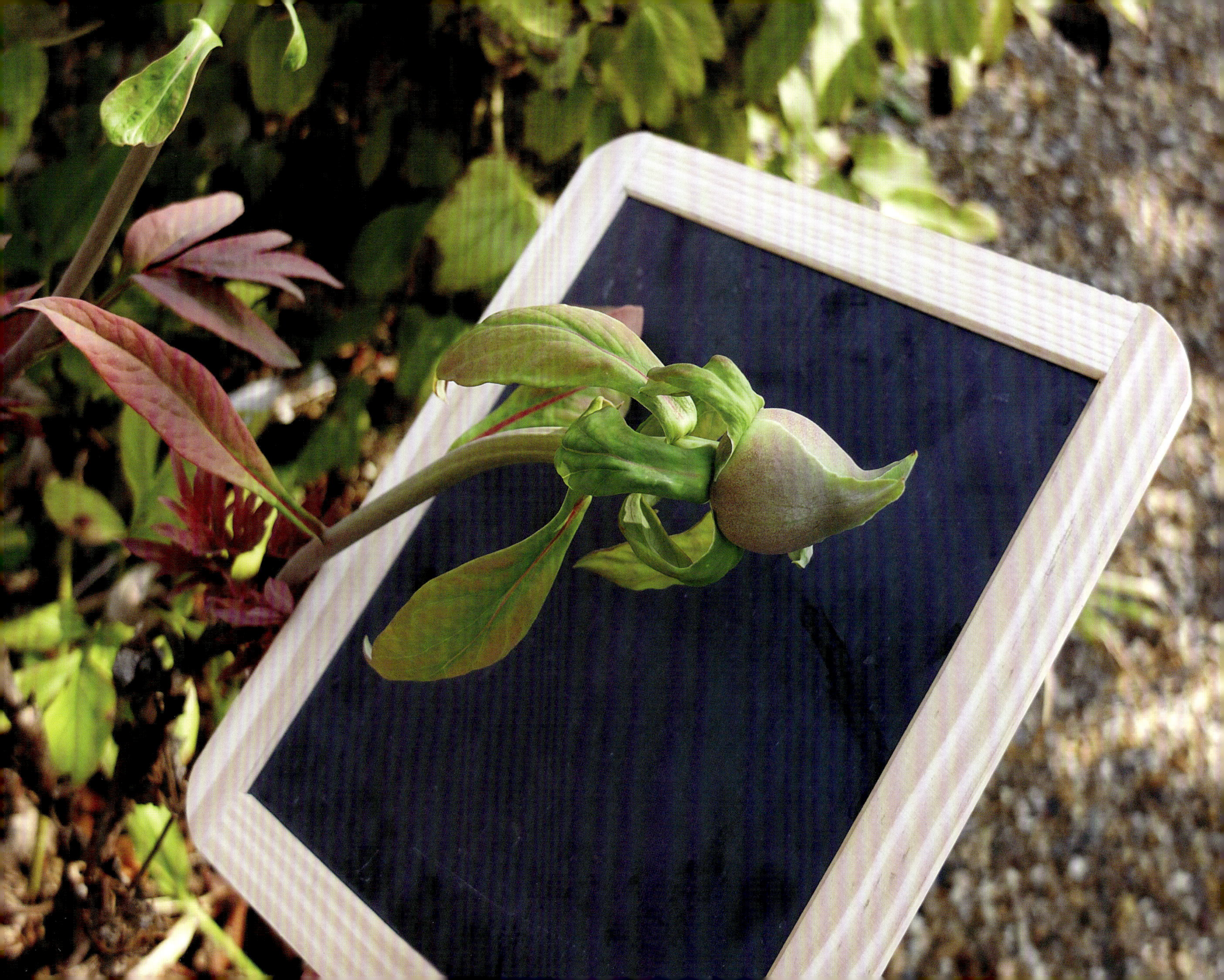

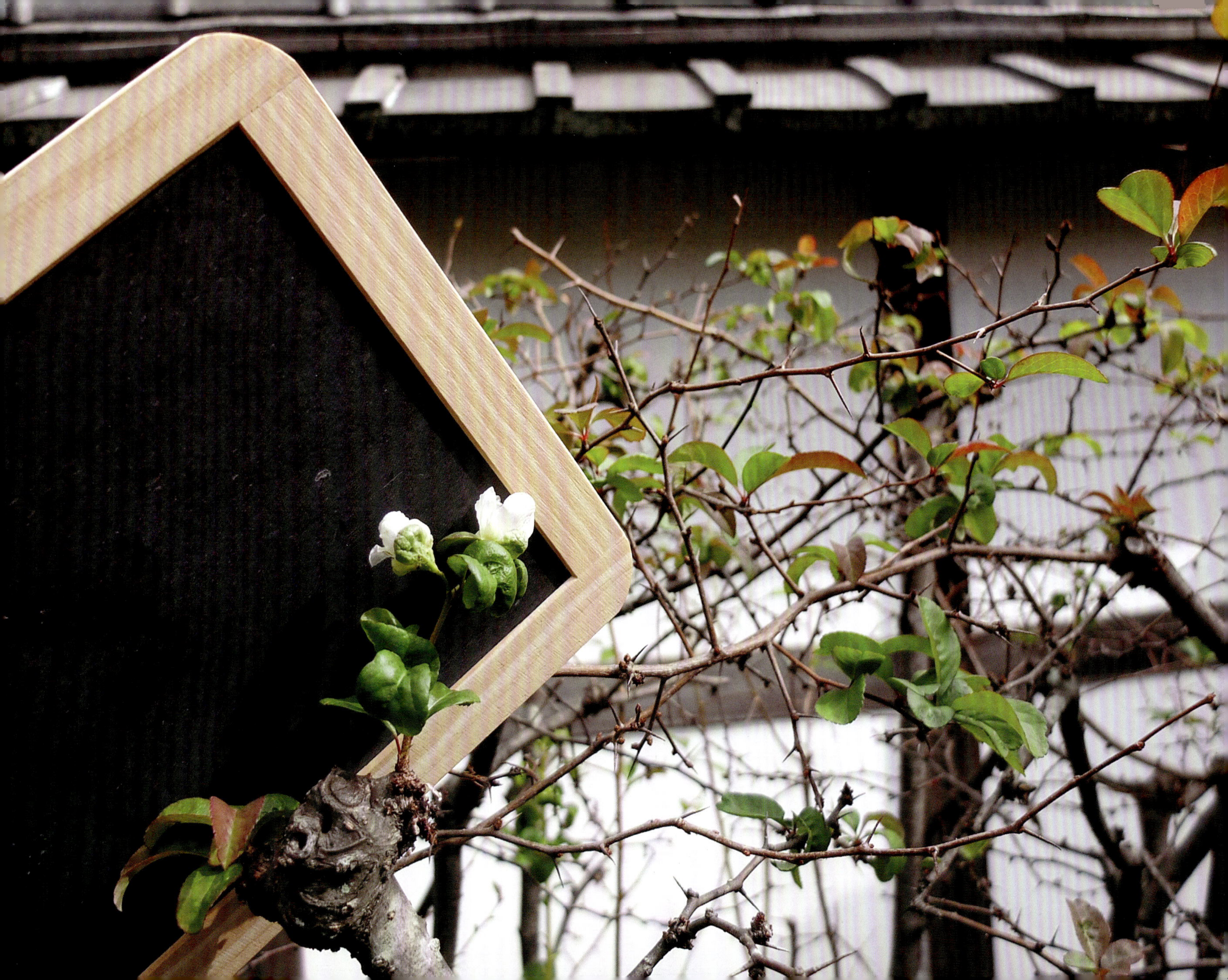

QUINCE

HANA KOTOBA : Good health, prosperity, commonplace
JAPANESE : *Karin*
GROWING CONDITIONS : Clay, heavy, well-drained soil.

At Kennin-ji, history and beauty mingled and caught my eye at every turn. The quince tempted me to touch it, but its thorny stem warned of intrusion. I liked the simplicity and gentle bearing of the flower adjacent to its own obstacle course. The flower is known to bloom from late winter past New Year's to spring. It is used as bonsai material because of its toughness and versatility.

The quince has spent thousands of years in Japan. I find its image painted on fans and scrolls in museums. When I use it on an altar, I carefully clip off all the thorns to minimize its sharpness.

The wood is used to build Buddhist altars, called *butsudan*. Some quince trees bear fruit; however, it takes a long time and much effort to make jam. Easier to enjoy is the quince lozenge, a savory treat.

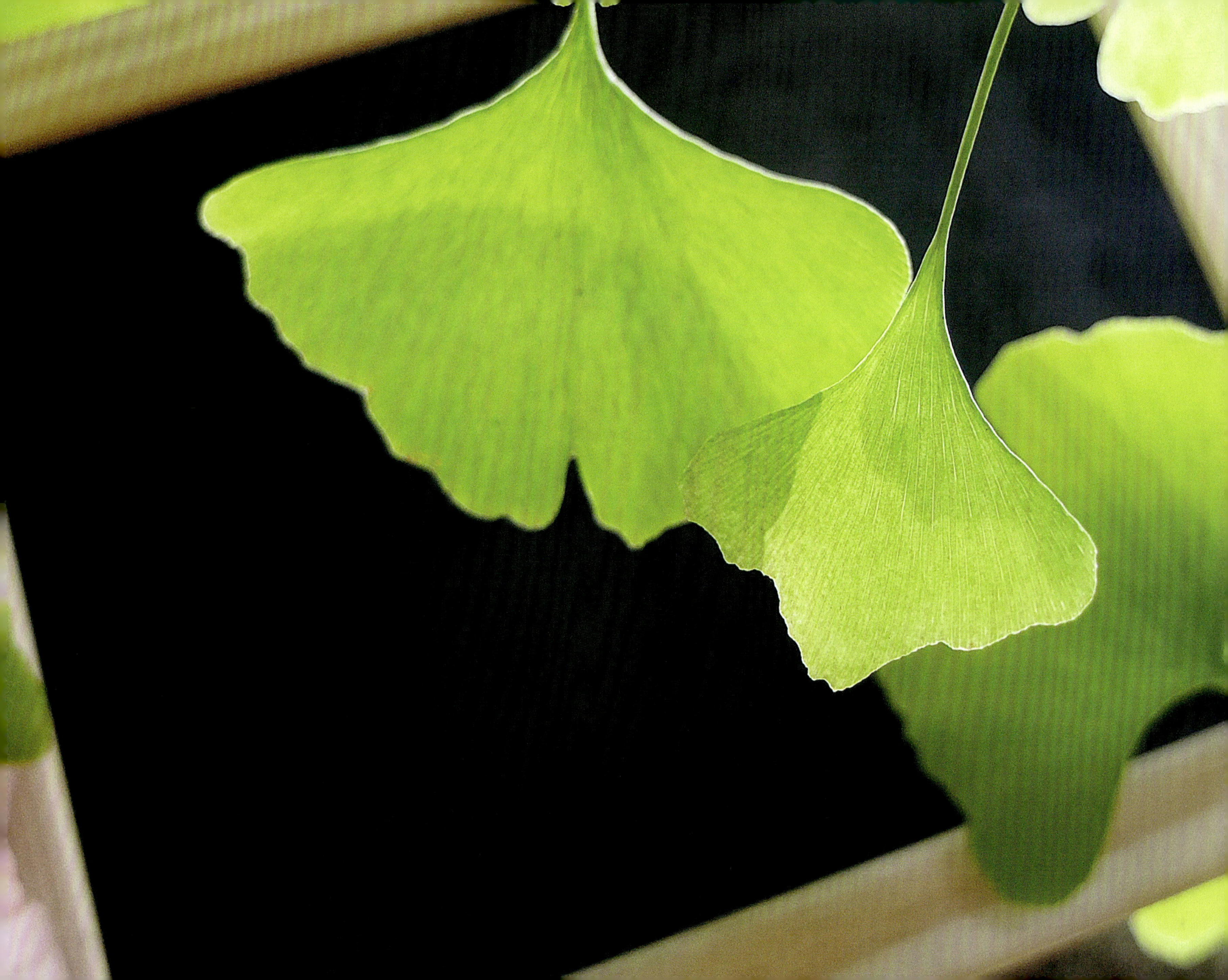

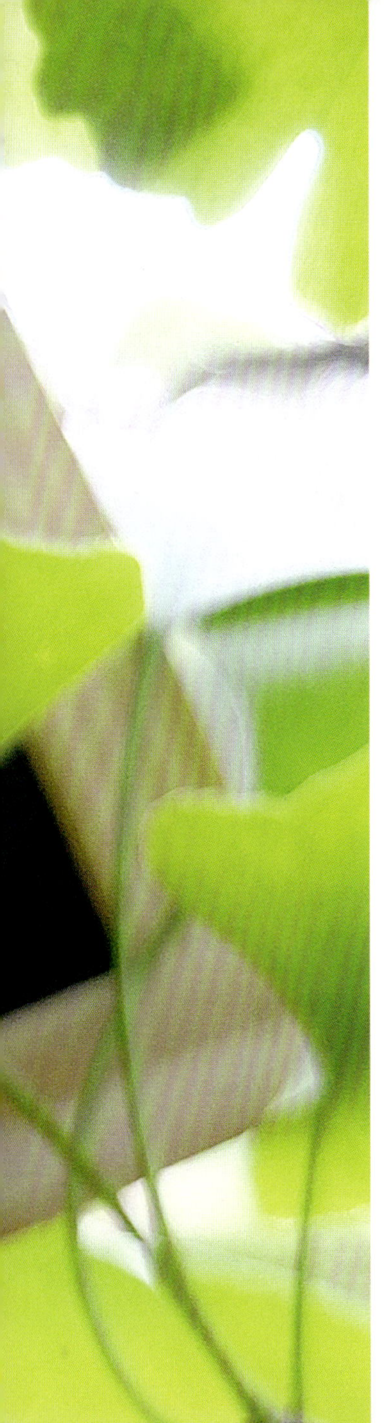

GINKGO

HANA KOTOBA : Longevity, profound endurance
JAPANESE : *Icho yin-hsing*
GROWING CONDITIONS : Sandy soil in full sun.

When I photographed this specimen in the Kyoto Botanical Gardens, the leaves were bright green and fresh as spring mint. I saw such a tree again in Kamakura at Tsurugaoka Hachimangū Shrine. In 1219, this tree provided cover for the assassin of the shogun Sanetomo. Its size and stoic presence arched over me as I stood underneath.

It is said that one's Buddhist practice is lifelong and almost invisible. The growing process of the ginkgo is long as well—a fraction of an inch each year. These leaves flutter together like an intimate sangha. It takes 20 years before a tree blooms from seed, and only then can the gender of the tree be certain.

Near Shinto shrines, there are old and respected ginkgos encircled with ropes and small white papers that mark where sacred spirits reside—they can measure 30 meters high. Four trees survived the Hiroshima blast and still grow today. Gratefully, temple gardens include ginkgoes that have saved the tree from extinction. Each leaf is unique, with a fan-shaped cleft making two lobes. In autumn, the color shifts to glowing yellow. If you are lucky enough to find the harvested wood, you can make lacquerware and abacus beads.

NANDINA, HEAVENLY BAMBOO

HANA KOTOBA : Domesticate, to move hardship or difficulty away, remove impurities
JAPANESE : *Nanten*
GROWING CONDITIONS : Sun or shade, better color in sun, indoor as well

No temple garden is complete without nandina. At Tenryū-ji the red berries of this plant were like exclamation dots on a page as I took a long view. The tree is traditionally described as "bearing red fruit like fire," and its berries can poison songbirds, and yet I sucked on throat candy made from nandina in the cold fall weather.

There are historical depictions and tales of samurai with this plant. The samurai referred to it as sacred bamboo, to clean their hands when there was no water or to ward off the negative effects of having a nightmare. They also believed that a switch of nandina would purify their mind or bring them good luck riding into battle. The tradition continues today with a branch tucked into a school child's lunchbox for good luck.

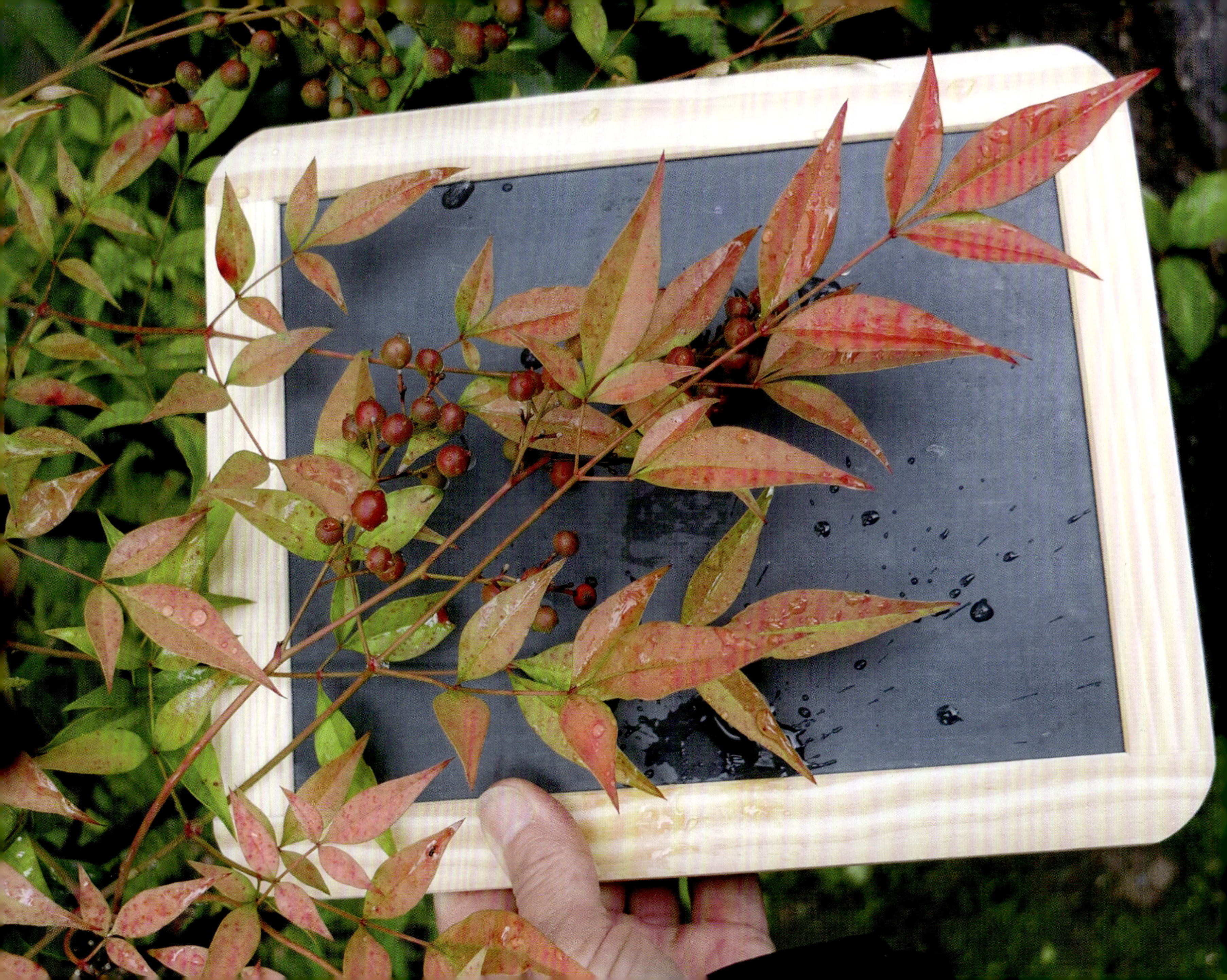

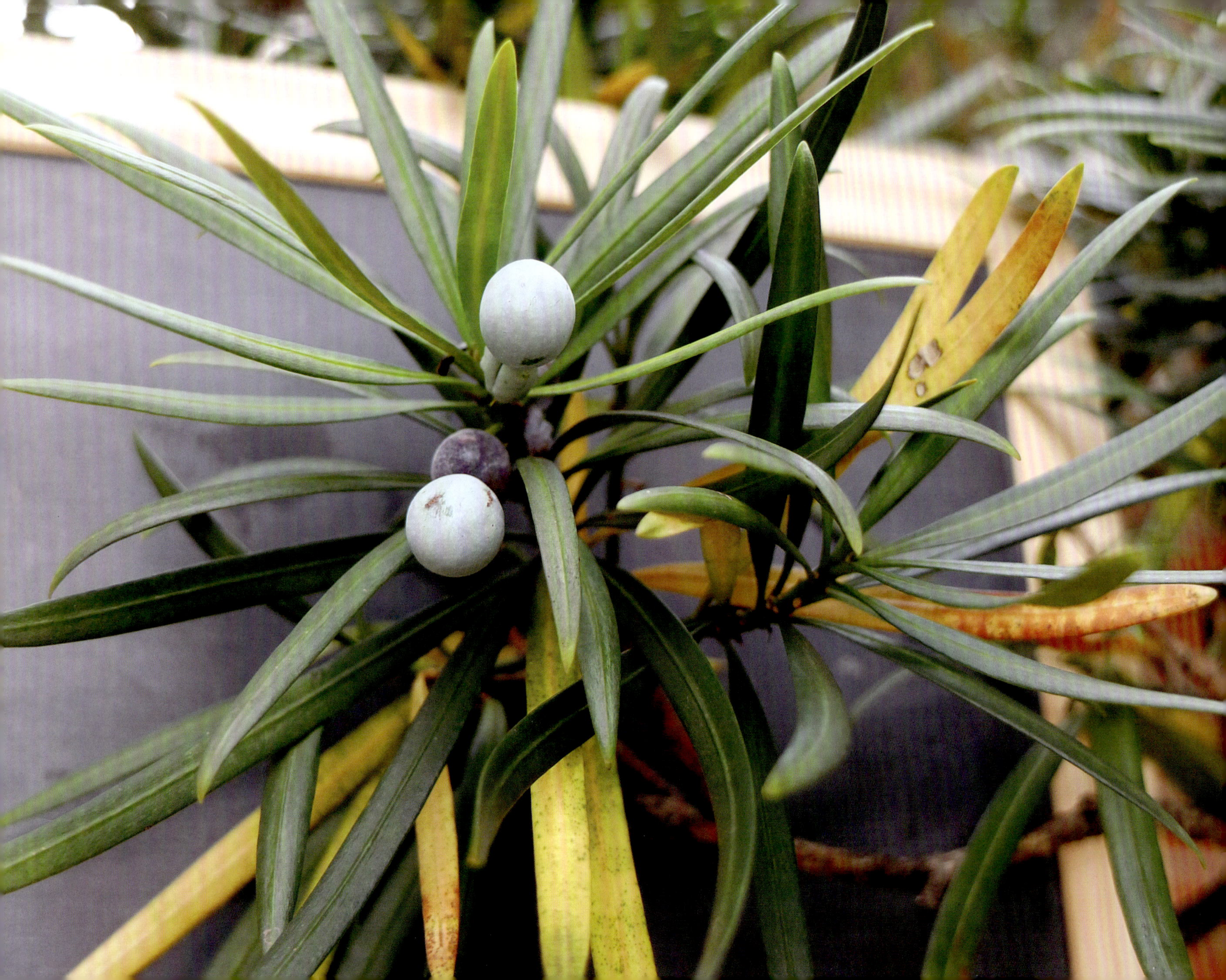

YEW PINE

HANA KOTOBA : Permanence, hope, longevity
JAPANESE : *Inumaki*
GROWING CONDITIONS : Shelter from wind, hot sun, and deep snow; grows slowly in tub.

This branch filled with colorful bursts of berries did not entice me, since the yews in Europe and the United States are decidedly poisonous. Here in Japan, they can be eaten and enjoyed.

Yews in these surroundings grow to be giant, 50-foot trees that have delicate branches that lean and float in the afternoon breeze with big berries dangling like bells.

Occasionally, the tree is called a Buddhist pine, and in China they are known as the *luohan*. This Buddhist term means *arhat*—a deified figure who has reached perfection through study and meditation. When Dogen spoke about "hearing" with the eye, he said, "This is the purity of a spring pine, the magnificence of an autumn chrysanthemum. Just this."

The berries of the yew pine in Japan are a favorite for pies and pastry and even to make a sweetened tonic.

WHITE CHRYSANTHEMUM

HANA KOTOBA : Purity, grief, truth, faithful wife
JAPANESE : *Kika*
GROWING CONDITIONS : Full sun, light soil, may freeze in cold winter; frequent pinching for a large bloom.

As I left Hirakata Park in Osaka, this giant single bloom, over five feet tall, greeted me at eye level as if to insist on its presence. Its shape and nobility reminded me of the golden altar emblems embroidered with the imperial crest. Not surprisingly, this chrysanthemum became the imperial seal of Japan. The monarchy is called the Chrysanthemum Throne.

As the sun was setting on the horizon, its golden light shone on the bloom, making it a magically stark white. Patience and great attention are essential to create one bloom from one plant, and there are more than 150 patterns of this design. Growing these regal flowers is a nationwide hobby, and in Tokyo there are competitions for the most prized and intricate bloom. Chrysanthemum Day is one of the five ancient sacred festivals, celebrated on the ninth day of the ninth month.

Dogen mentioned chrysanthemums in a poem:

Last year on the ninth month, leaving this place.
This year on the ninth month, coming from this place.
Stop dwelling on passing days, months, and years.
Look with delight in the undergrowth where chrysanthemums bloom.

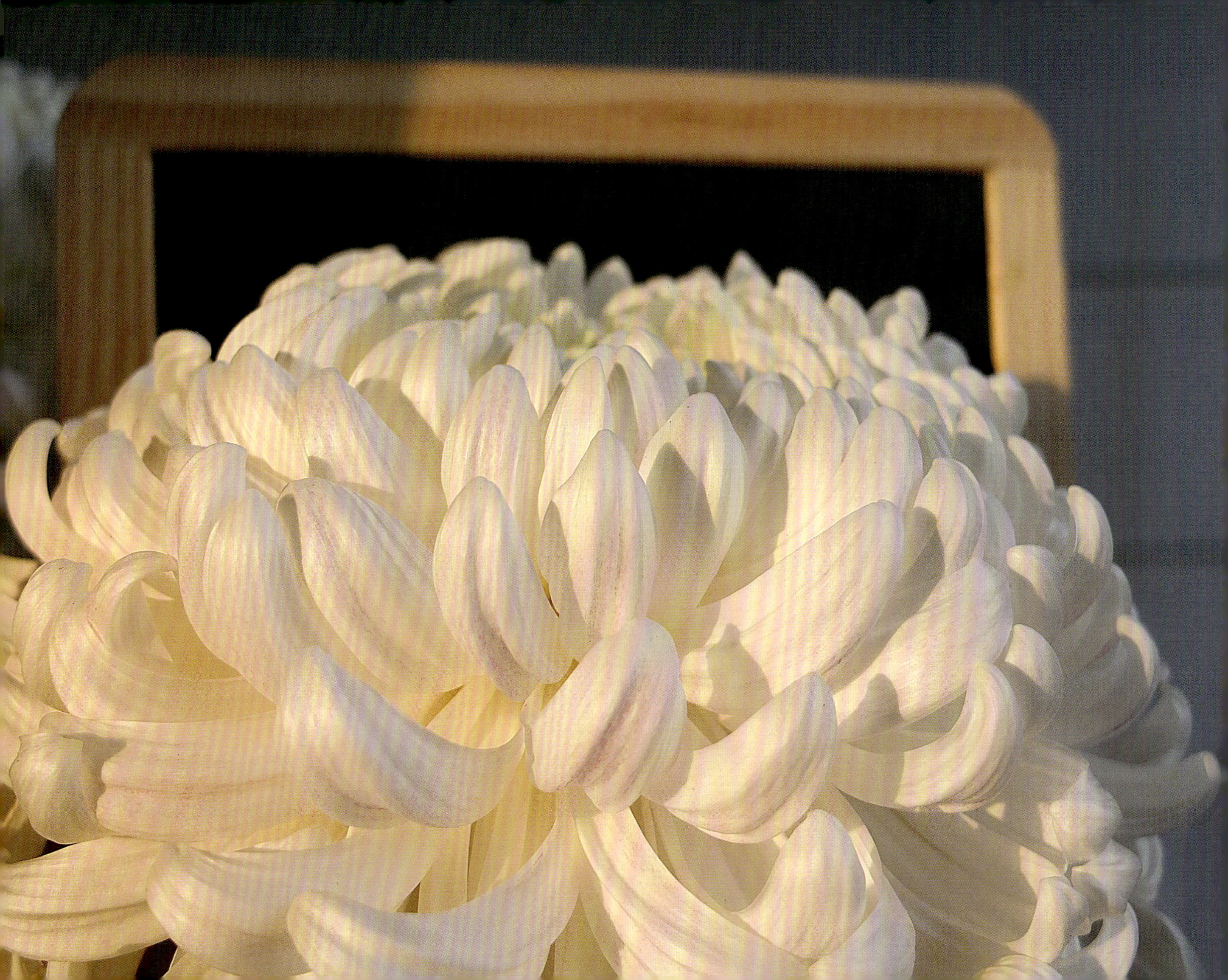

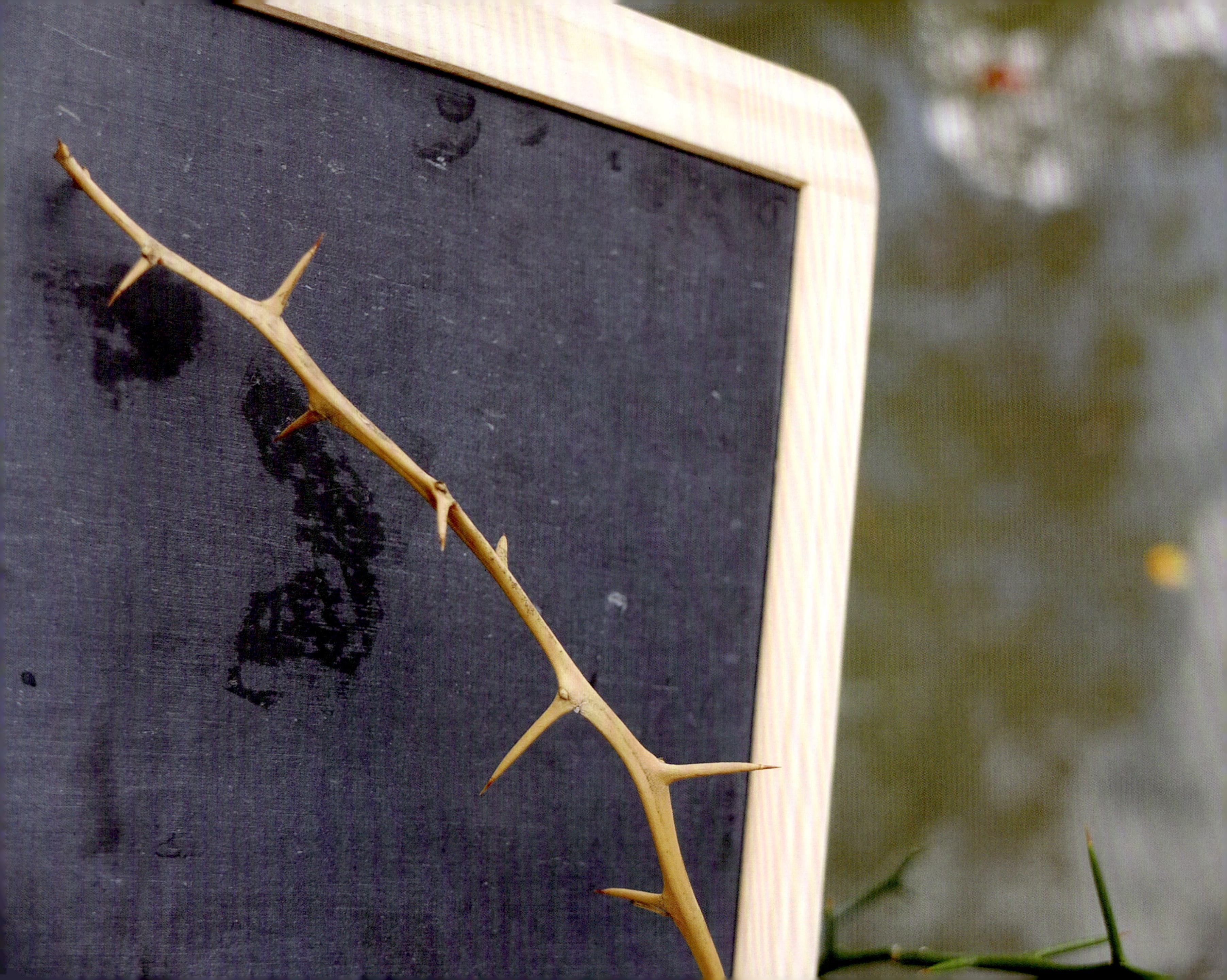

ROSA INDICA

HANA KOTOBA : Relief that a misfortune did not turn to tragedy (thorns)
JAPANESE : *Momoirobara*
GROWING CONDITIONS : Full sun, air circulates freely.

Perhaps it was the sense of season that made me photograph this rose in such a stark way. Without color or gentle petals, the branch made this plant feel skeletal and bare like a winter poem.

When incense isn't allowed at an altar, torn rose petals are used for an offering. During the celebration of Buddha's birthday, we dip our fingers into baskets filled with rose petals to scatter and toss them up in the air. By the end of the last chant, the room is filled with their sweet, enchanting smell.

The rose isn't a favorite fragrance in Japan. But it can be used for perfume or rosewater. Mostly it is just enjoyed on the stem in nature or in a simple vase.

CHINESE JUNIPER

HANA KOTOBA : Great journey
JAPANESE : *Kaizuka ibuki*
GROWING CONDITIONS : Every type of soil; keep roots dry.

Kennin-ji is the oldest temple in Kyoto. On the grounds are seven ancient juniper trees called *byakushin*. Everywhere on the tree are berries, which take 18 months to mature from blue to black. The ancestor of this plant is known as "heaven on earth."

In the 13th century, Dogen lived and studied here and began to promote the practice of zazen. This juniper could very well have been one he strolled under during good weather. Courtyards and juniper trees are part of koan history in Buddhism. A famous koan includes "the juniper tree in the garden"—a response made by Joshu when asked the meaning of Bodhidharma's coming from the West. Trees are wonderful metaphors in Buddhist writing, and this particular juniper has been written about in hundreds of books.

It is mostly the berries that are of use—birds love them and medicinal tinctures are made from them. Shōdō Harada Rōshi commented about "the uselessness of the Chinese juniper for lumber or nearly any other purpose."

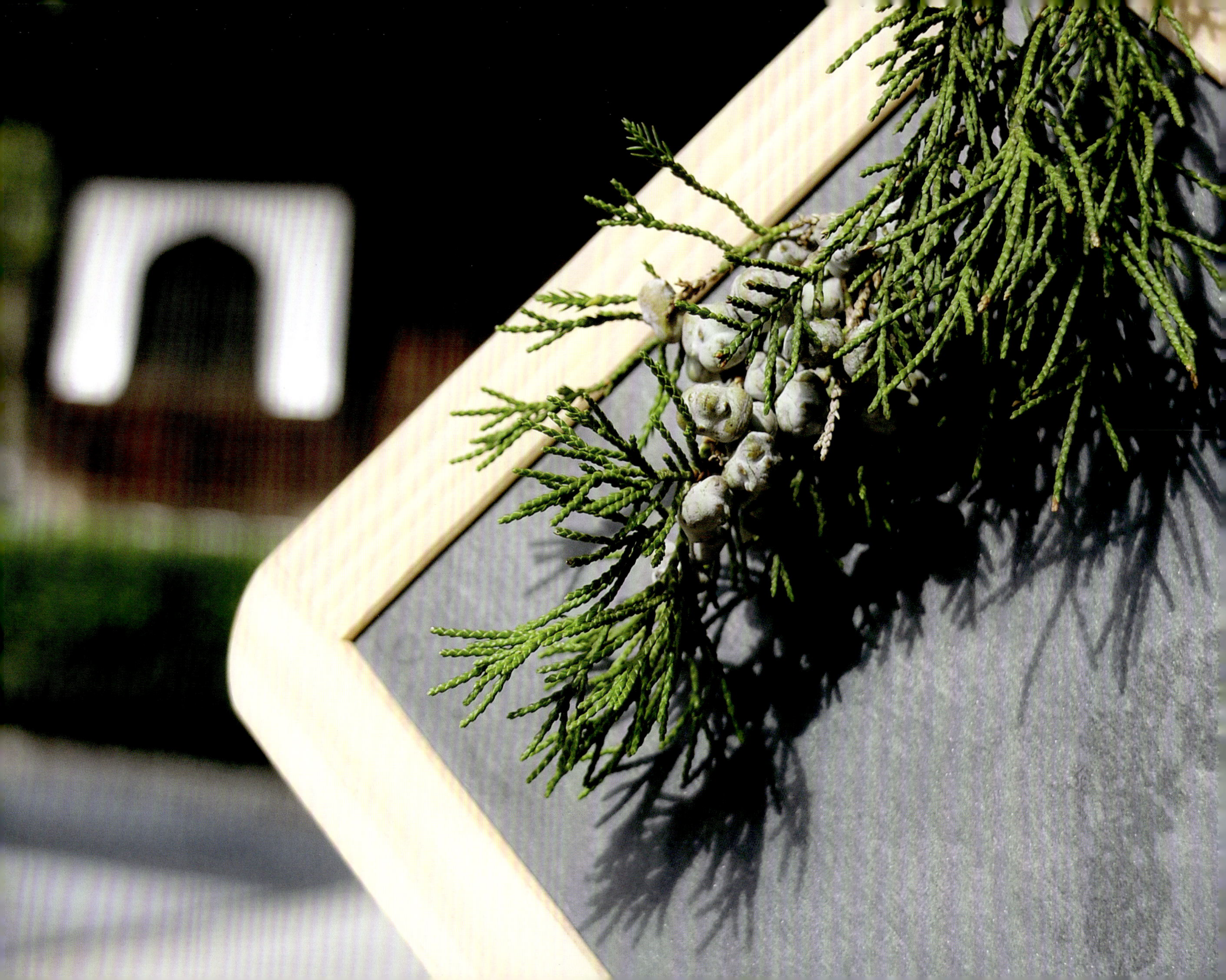

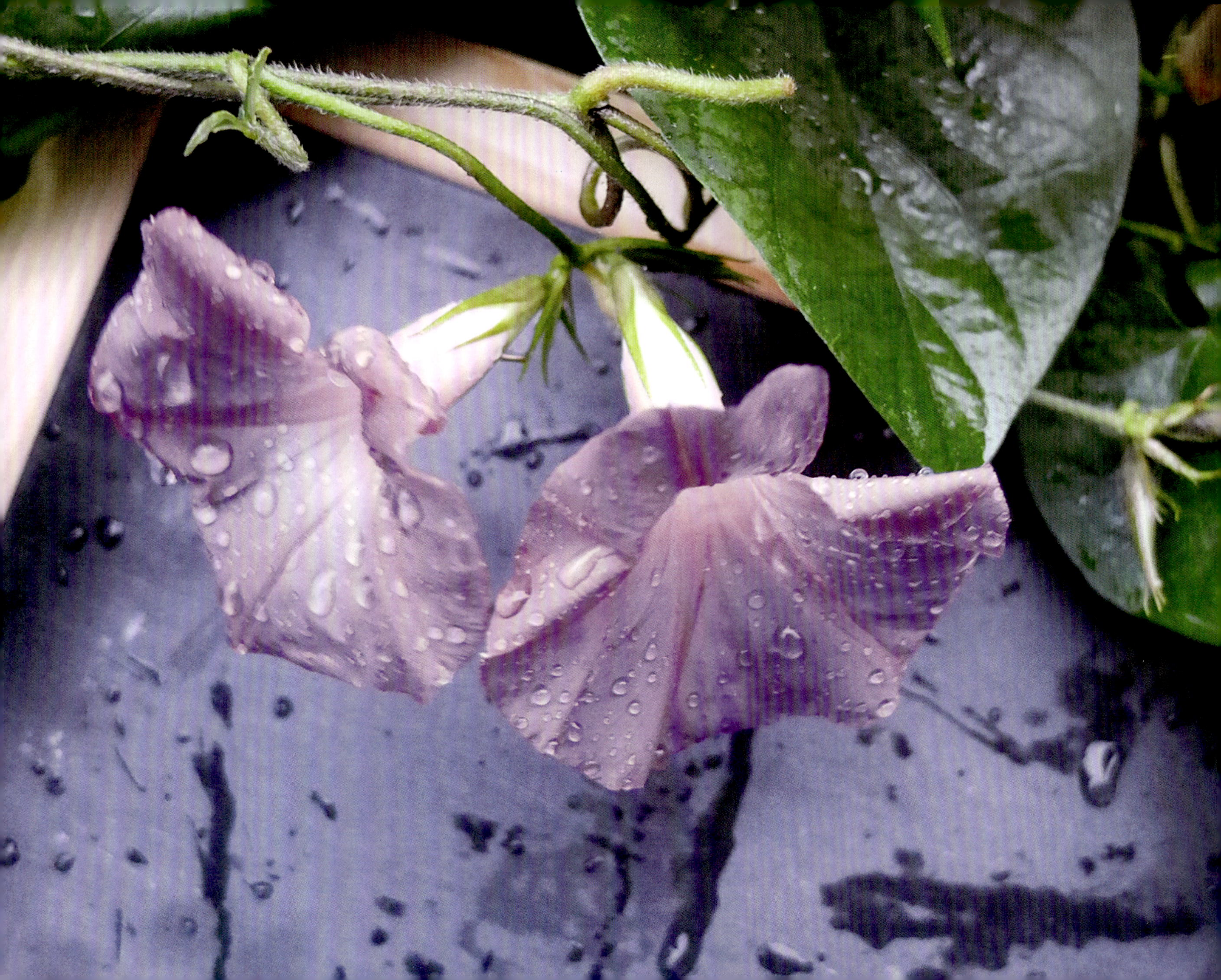

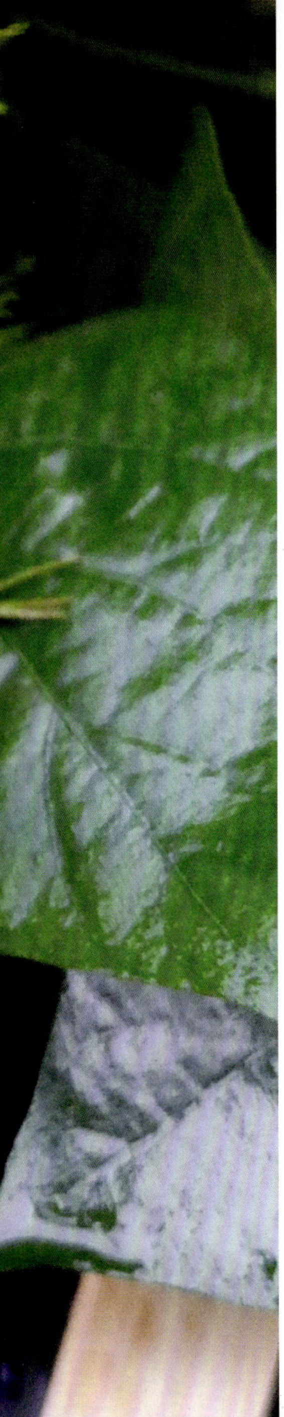

MORNING GLORY

HANA KOTOBA : Willful promises, attachment
JAPANESE : *Asagao*
GROWING CONDITIONS : Full sun, light soil, fast drainage, protect from overhead watering.

In the early hours of sunrise, I walked through neighborhoods where front doorways included pots of morning glories to liven up the new day. The morning dew sparkled on the tender petals.

Dogen referred to dew in his writing, especially the moon reflected in a dewdrop. The short life of the morning glory has the same sensibility as this observation of his:

Students today should begrudge every moment of time. This dew-like life fades away; time speeds swiftly. In this short life of ours, avoid involvement in superfluous things and just study the Way.

Perhaps the front-door entry is a good place to be reminded of this idea.

Arranged blooms last longer if cut while still wet with dew. The seeds have value as a laxative.

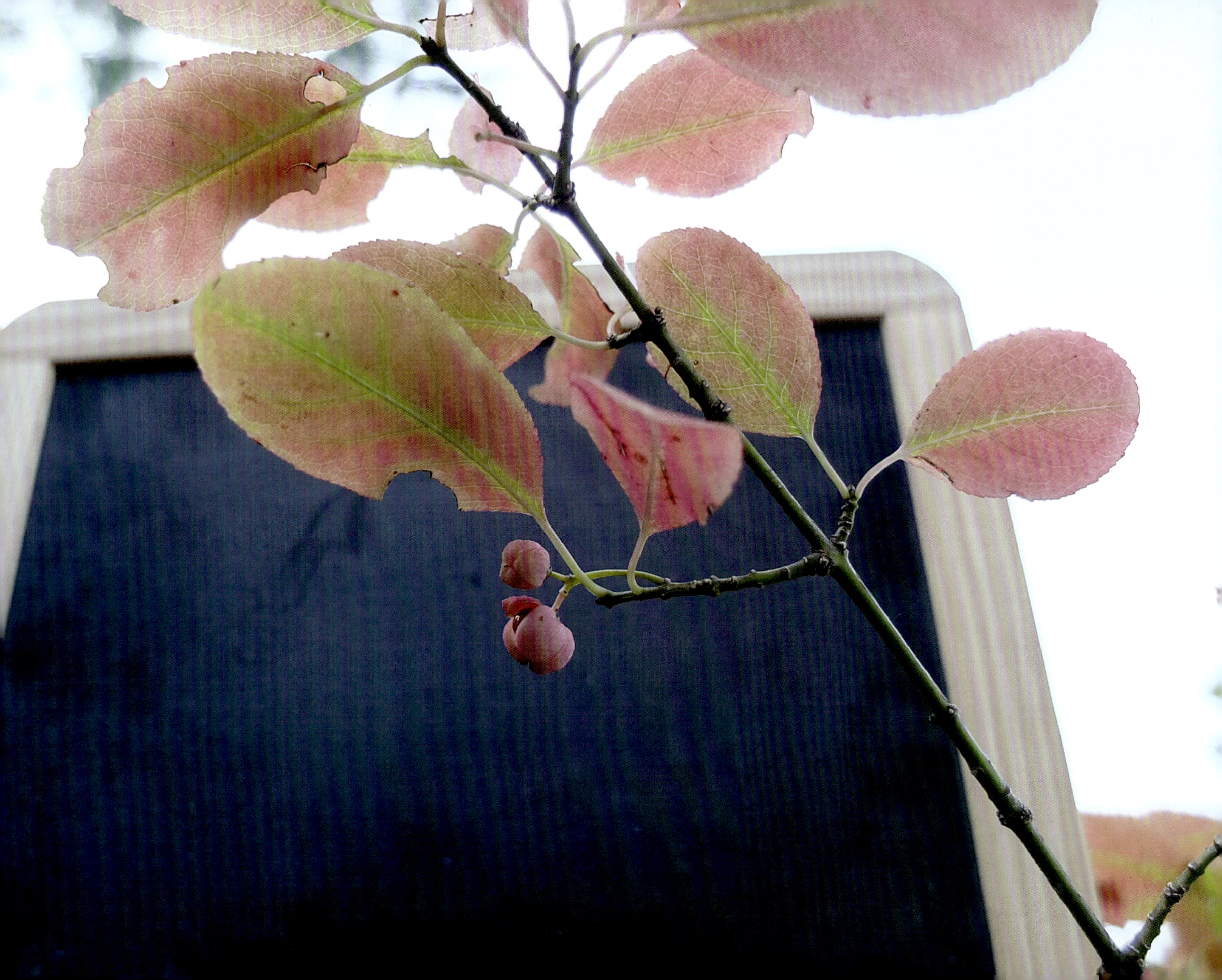

CHINESE SPINDLE TREE

HANA KOTOBA : A long time, but not eternity
JAPANESE : *Mayumi*
GROWING CONDITIONS : Moist, well-drained soil; dappled shade, morning sun.

The arboretum's afternoon light glistened over these *mayumi* leaves, making them semi-transparent and enchanting. The fruits have lids that spring open, inviting birds to come by for the delectable orange seeds. Depending on the season, the foliage can be red, pink, or yellow.

In years past and sometimes now, abbots have walked with staffs made from the dense wood of the spindle tree. The wood's strength and compactness make it a good choice.

In the Nezu Museum in Tokyo, there is a famous tea caddy called the "spindle tree," as the amber glaze is the same color as the vines on the tree. Look for it in ikebana arrangements, archery bows, and inlay.

This tree is also used in medicinal preparations, primarily as a purgative, although careful attention must be paid because some are poisonous to humans.

JAPANESE AUCUBA

HANA KOTOBA : None

JAPANESE : *Aoki*

GROWING CONDITIONS : Deep shade, slow growing, can compete with tree roots.

The nice thing about the aucuba is that it lives in unexpected shady places. I found this one in a forest of sugi trees nestled in the darkness, happy to be there. Its streaks of variegated gold or yellow brighten any spot in a garden. Even on a pitch-black night, its self-illuminated leaves resonate a presence like little guideposts.

Add to this the characteristic of being a sturdy plant that thrives in the most difficult of garden environments, and the aucuba is a good choice for many gardeners. This male plant doesn't have berries, but the wild splashes of yellow make up for it.

Sometimes, in the long hours of meditation, I yearn for the stamina of the aucuba.

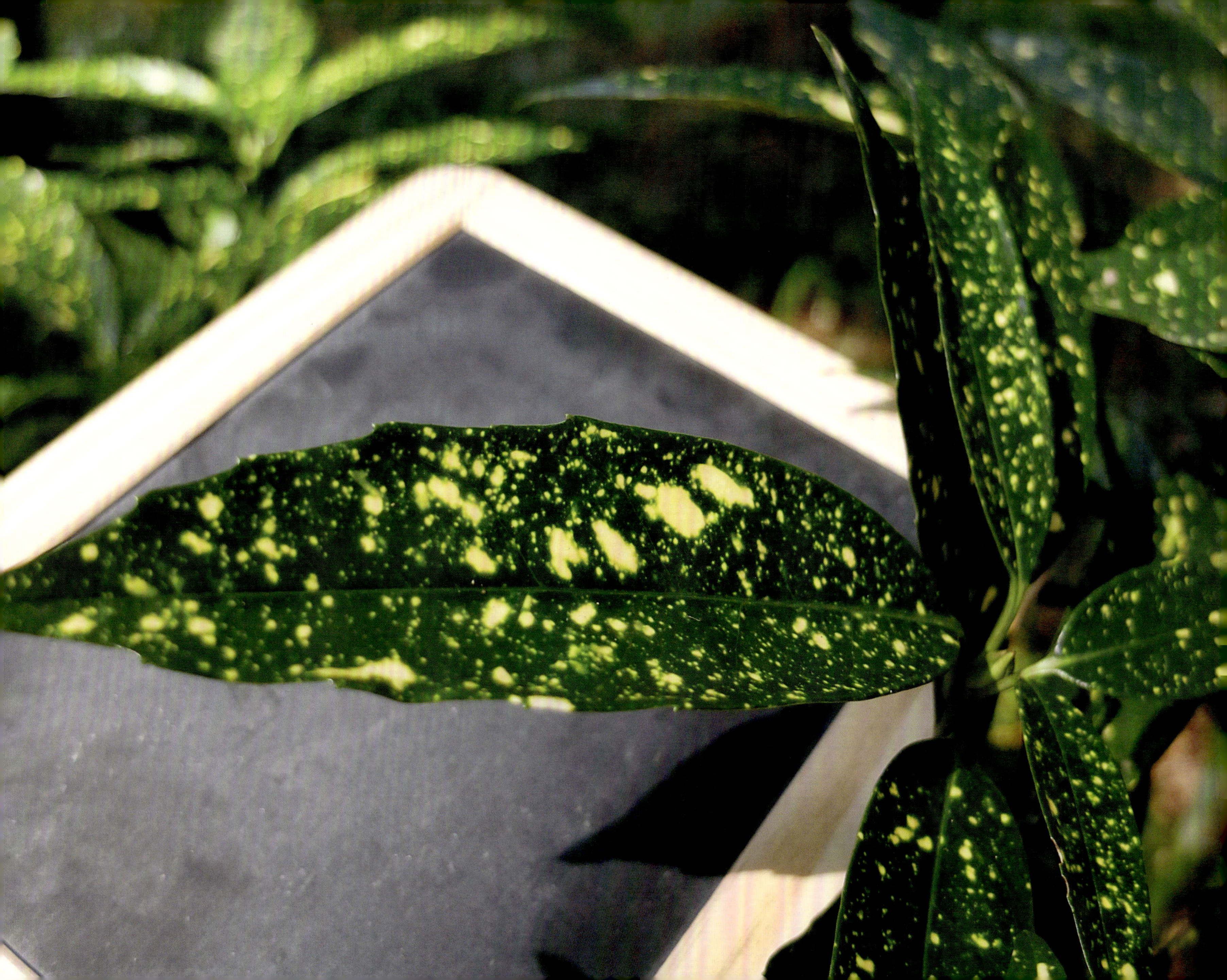

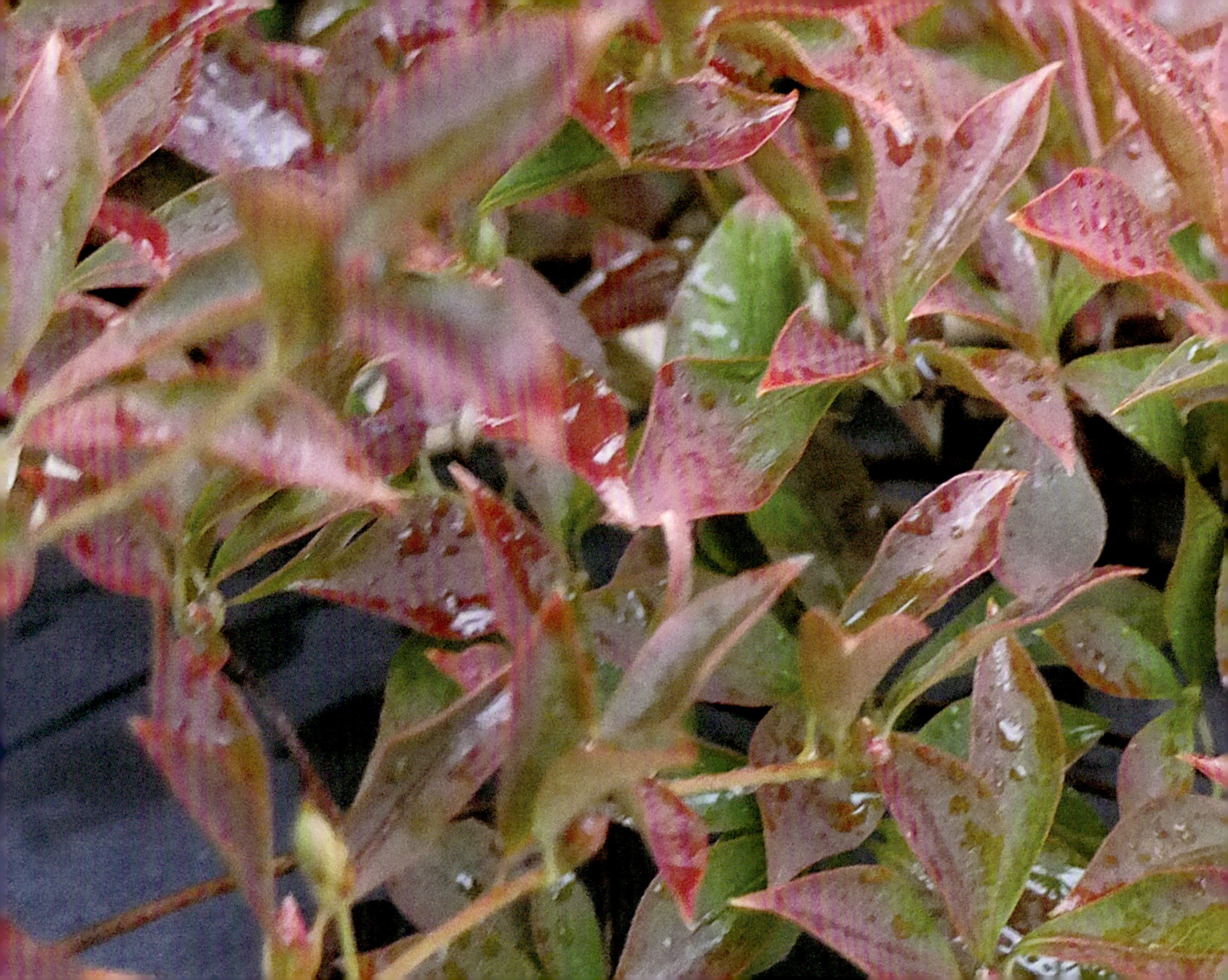

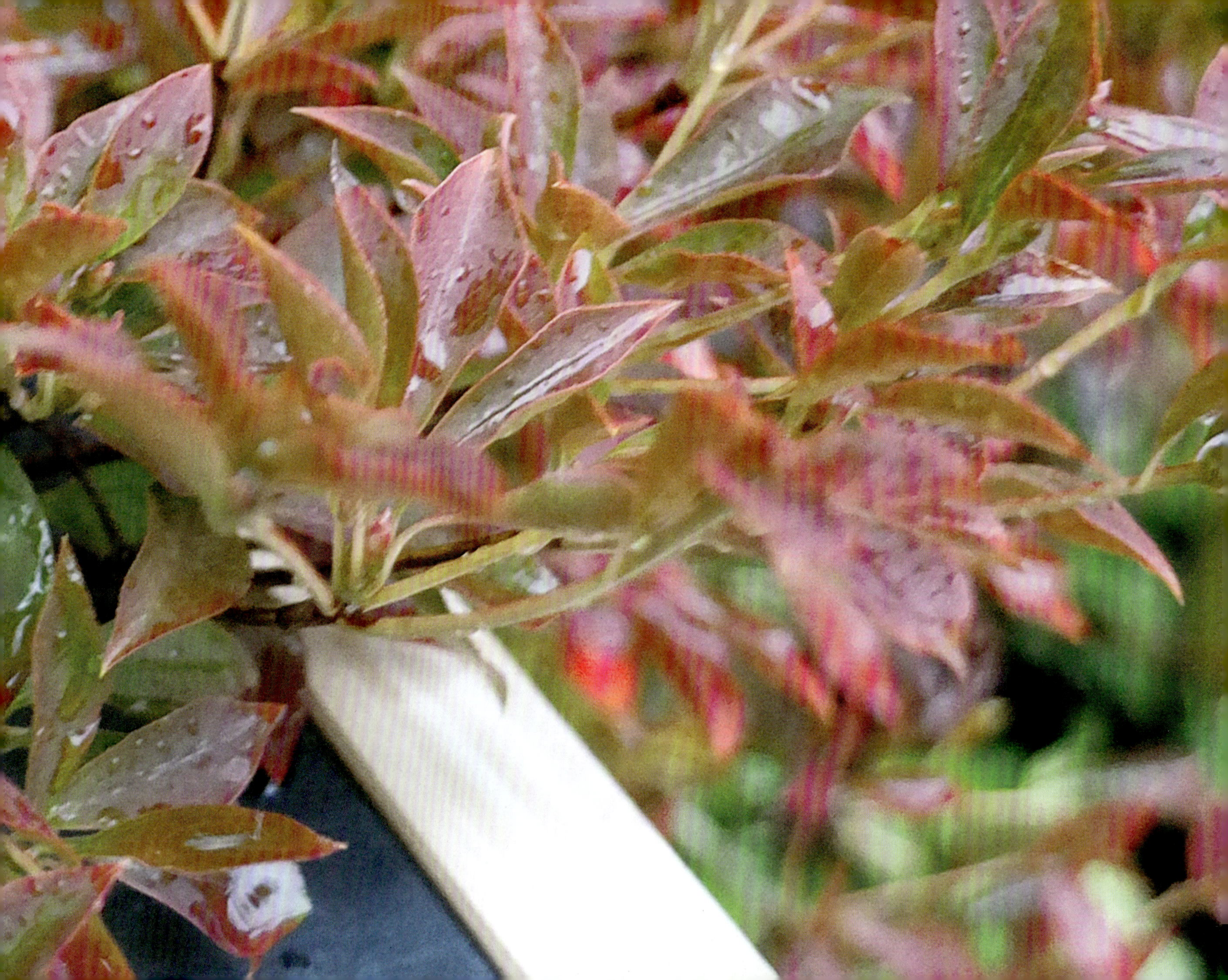

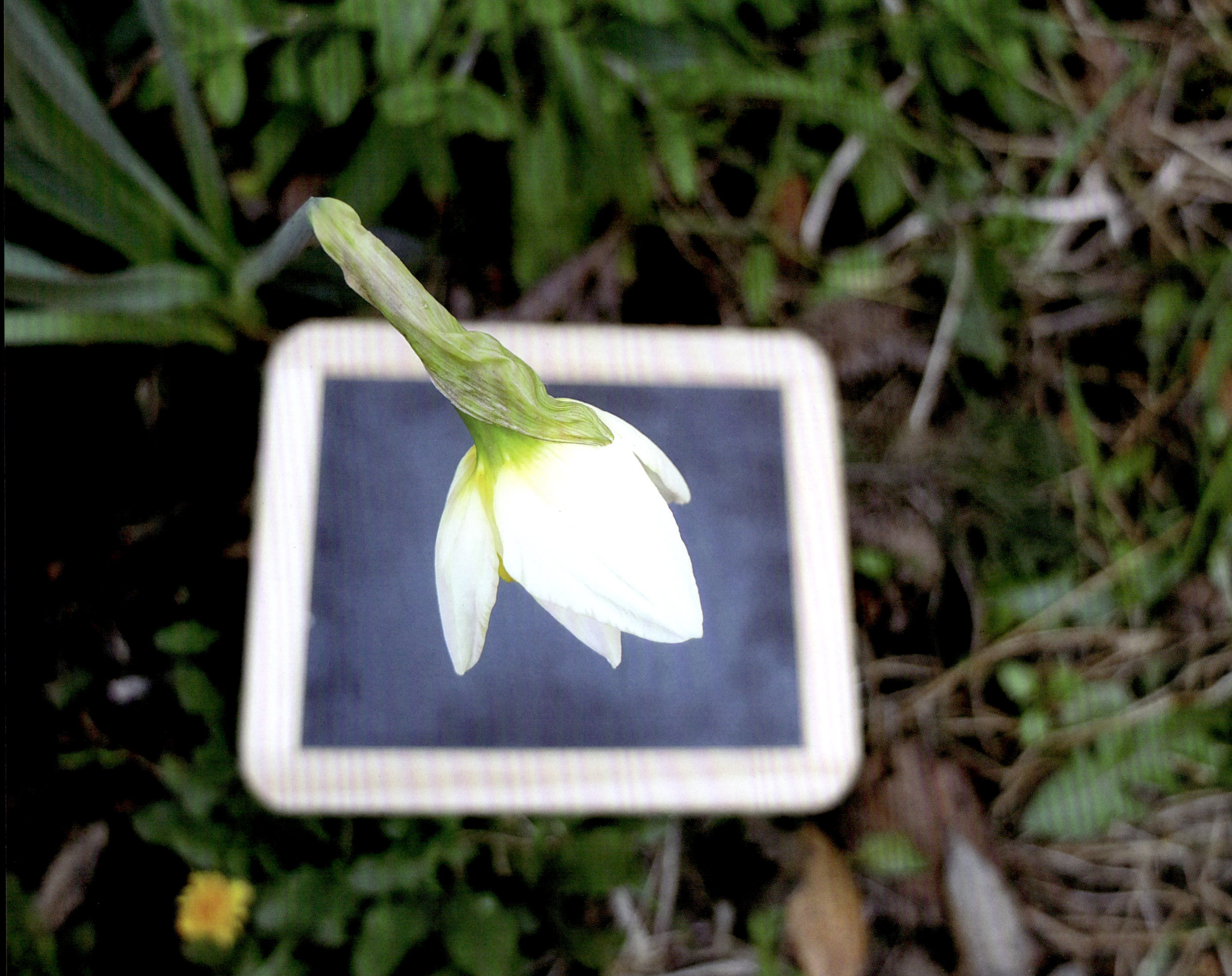

CHINESE NARCISSUS

HANA KOTOBA : Self-esteem, good fortune
JAPANESE : *Suisen*
GROWING CONDITIONS : Limestone soil that keeps dry in summer, a mixed wild forest.

When I came across this bloom, I knew winter was waning. She popped up neat and clean in an open field, sitting solitary like a shy flower with its color still sheltered from my eye.

Her posture, curving downward, made me think of eyes partially closed while sitting in zazen. Imagine the valiant effort it takes to push up from below the ground amid layers of stones, earth, and other life.

Known as a water wizard in Japan, this 700-year-old plant carries Indian and Buddhist doctrine in its history. To offer such a flower is a gesture of respect—it is said the samurai favored this sentiment.

CREPE MYRTLE

HANA KOTOBA : Unpreparedness
JAPANESE : *Sarusuberi*
GROWING CONDITIONS : Moist soil in early stages.

The Kyoto Botanical Gardens are like an encyclopedia of Japanese flowers. With patience, I can see almost every species here. I stopped before the crepe myrtle in silent reverence; it is the longest-blooming tree in existence, the bloom lasting 60 to 120 days. But that's not all. Then it bursts into a wild theater of yellow, orange, and red leaves. No wonder it is popular for nesting songbirds longing for an extended vacation. Its brilliant red blooms make an exotic home for extroverted warblers.

The Japanese name, *sarusuberi*, translates to "the monkey slips," referring to the myrtle's perilously slippery branches.

The impermanence of the leaves, changing color and dropping to the ground, is bolder to me than a Buddhist monk.

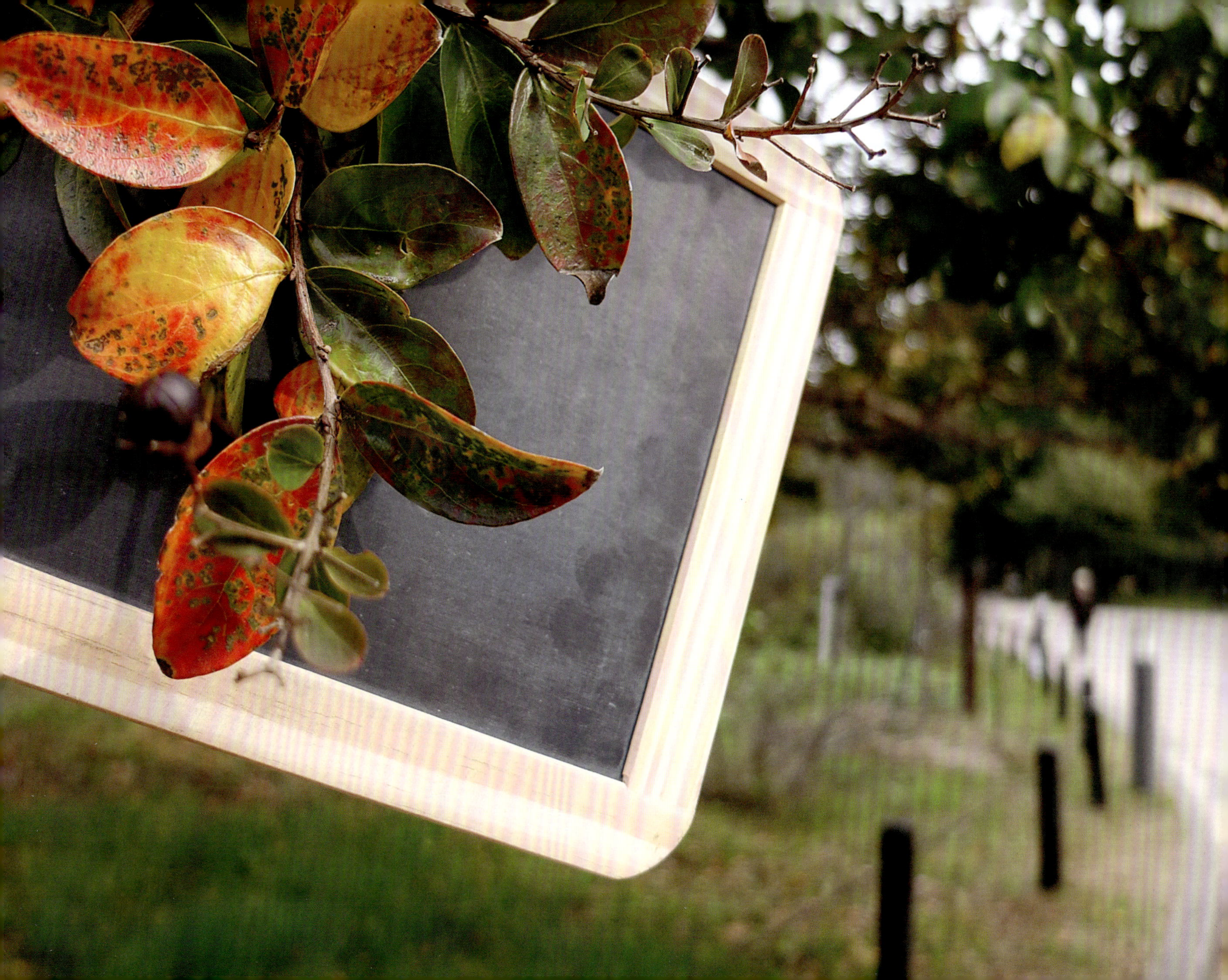

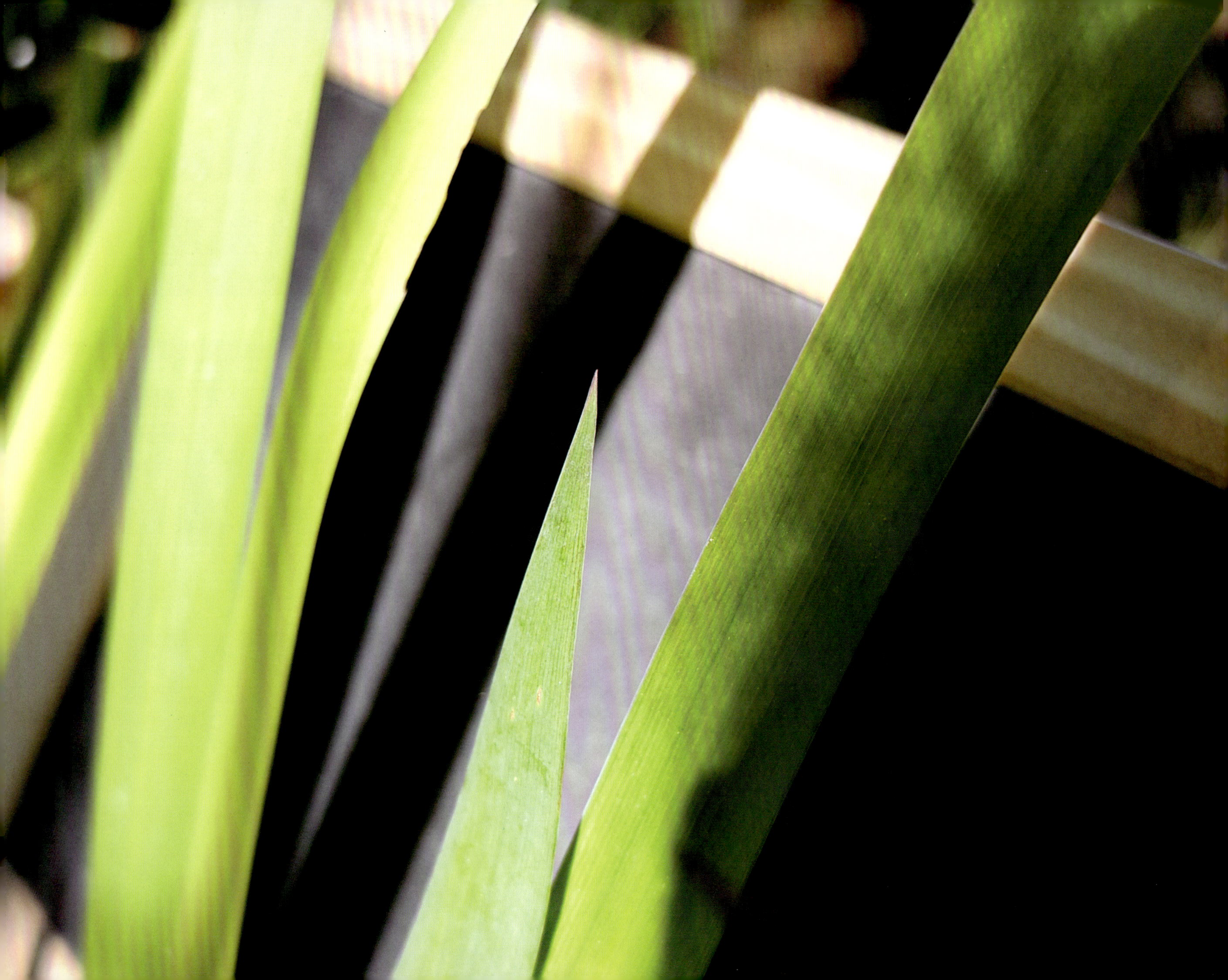

JAPANESE IRIS

HANA KOTOBA : Elegant spirit

JAPANESE : *Hanashōbu*

GROWING CONDITIONS : Waterside, full sun.

The iris has a short burst of color, and then it looks like a symbol of courage with its bold, sharp leaves resembling Japanese swords. I was told that this plant is able to purify evil energies and protect those who wear the leaf. Wearing it is somewhat of a challenge because of its size and shape, although a kimono with an iris design flamboyantly enlivens the cloth. In some places in Japan, you might also see it hanging under the eaves of houses to drive away the spirits.

Basho, a Japanese poet, wrote in 1688 a haiku about the iris's swift demise to honor a friend whose sudden death surprised him.

Motome—
Iris withered
only in one night

On Children's Day in the spring, iris leaves are used in a bath (*shoubu-yu*) to ward off plague with its fragrance. It's a day to respect and celebrate the personality of each child. The stems also connote straightforwardness—a characteristic that is highly encouraged in Buddhist practice.

JAPANESE BEAUTYBERRY

HANA KOTOBA : None

JAPANESE : *Shiroshikibu*

GROWING CONDITIONS : Full sun, average water, wild in wooded countryside.

Near the edge of a serene pond, these upright beautyberry branches flowed elegantly like arches toward the water. My eye followed their directive as if I, too, were drawn to its stillness.

This shrub bears the name of Murasaki Shikibu, the author and main character of *The Tale of Genji*, a book about a beautiful consort who told the story of the inner life of the Imperial Court and allowed us to see behind the closed gate. No doubt exquisite purple and pink berries added to the enticement.

In Dogen's garden, the branches point to nearby areas, emphasizing a place of peace like this contemplative pond. Today, birds continue to enjoy the beautyberry's placement in a calm ambiance.

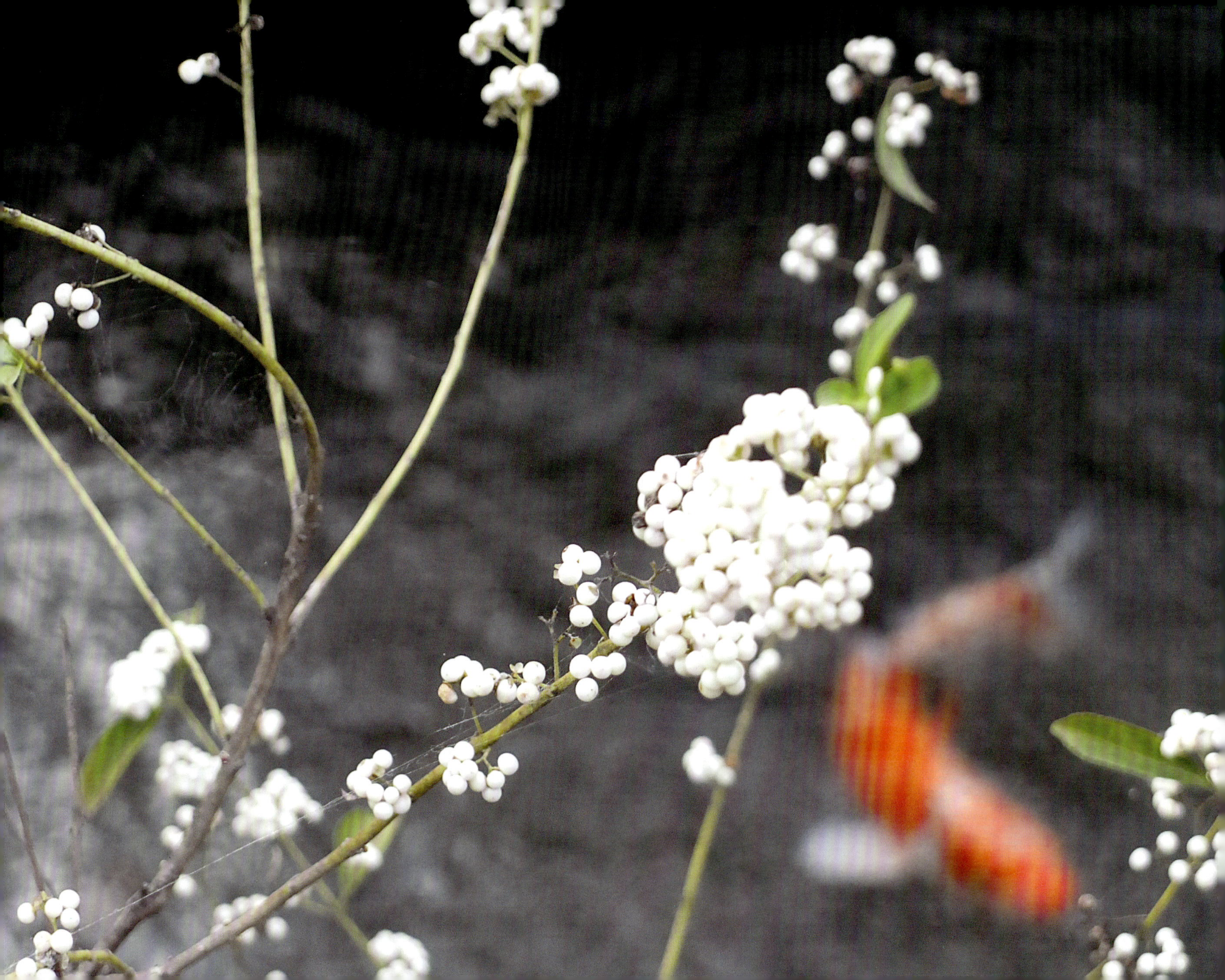

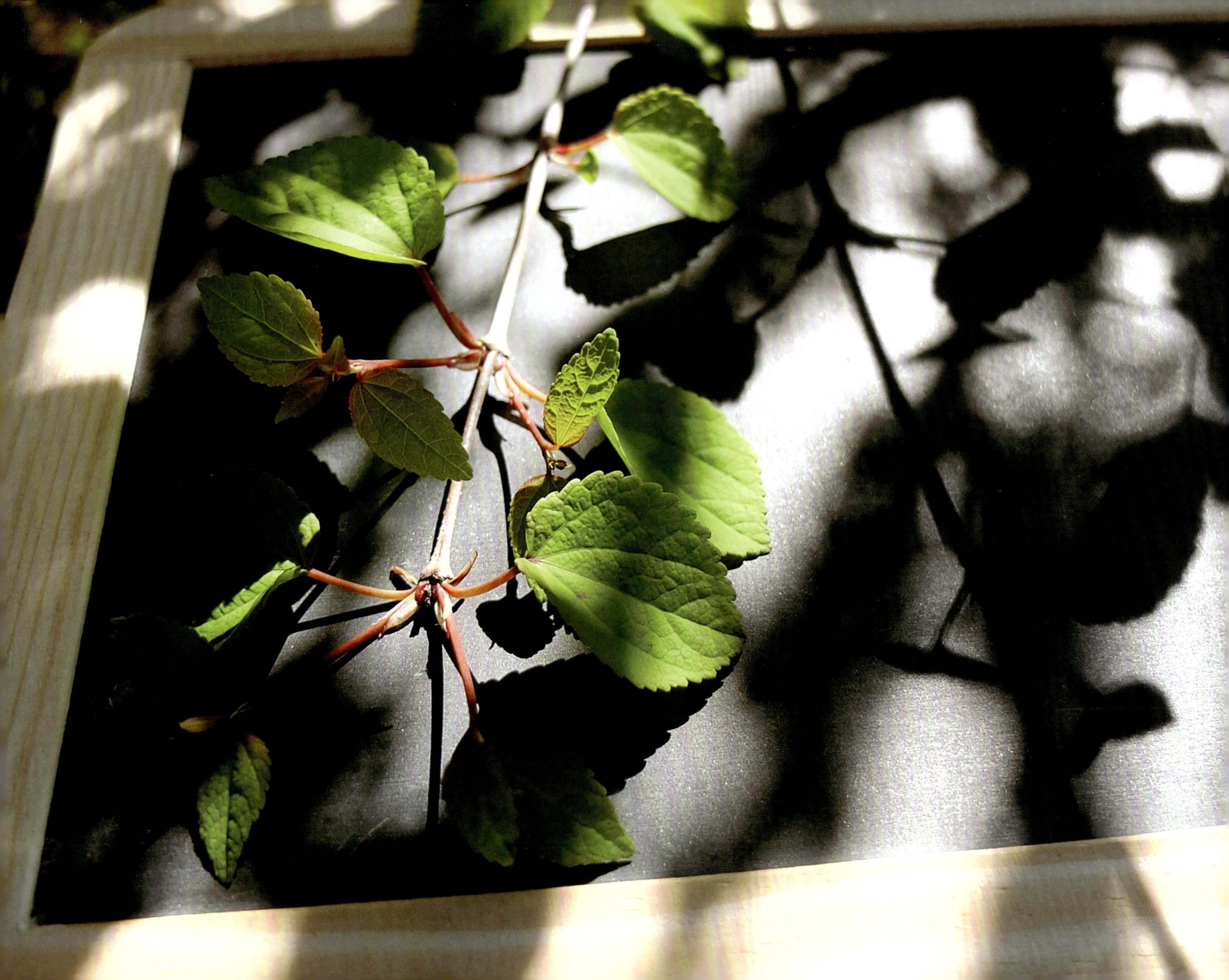

KATSURA TREE

HANA KOTOBA : None

JAPANESE : *Katsura*

GROWING CONDITIONS : Deep, permanently loose, moist soil. Grows in woodlands.

This young tree was hidden in a grove of larger trees. I noticed the symmetry of the leaves and knew it was a katsura. This leaf pattern is particular to the tree. If I had revisited it in the fall, I would have enjoyed the strong, sweet aroma of brown sugar.

The branches seemed to twirl like dancers in the summer breeze. Its ancestors come from Morioka, Japan. This is a tree you can visit often, since it changes with each season—the summer green pictured here, or reddish purple in spring, or yellow-apricot in fall. When the leaves are swept in the fall, their fragrance is like cotton candy.

Harvested wood is used to make the Go board called a goban. The aim of a player in this game is to surround more territory than the opponent. Go was introduced to Japan in the 11th century, and the rings of the katsura tree create a tigerish design on the board. Dogen used Go to make a point as he paraphrased Wanshi, a Chinese Zen master:

"Discussing this is like two players playing Go, where you've got to answer my move if you don't want to get taken for a ride."

An ancient Japanese folktale says that the shadow on the moon was created when a man being punished by the gods was sentenced to cut down a giant katsura tree on the moon. The shadow we see belongs to this tree. And as for the man, he is trapped on the moon forever.

CHERRY

HANA KOTOBA : Fleeting beauty, brevity of life
JAPANESE : *Sakura*
GROWING CONDITIONS : Full sun, fast-draining soil. Prune as little as possible.

In the temple garden at Uji, cherry blossoms floated down to the ground around my feet like pink butterflies. They reminded me of a tradition of mine at home: each spring my dog, Figaro, and I would lie on a blanket under a cherry tree and watch the pink blooms gently drift onto my face and his black coat.

Cherry blossoms are transient beauties that last only two weeks. This brief window creates much excitement in Japan. In fact, the tradition to enjoy cherry blossoms is called *hanami*, which also coincides with rice-planting season.

A favorite myth tells the marriage story of the cherry blossom princess, Sakuya-Hime. Her father, the god of Mount Fuji, wanted the suitor, Ninigi, to marry Sakuya's sister (the rock princess), but he refused. Instead of choosing the princess of long-lasting stones, he chose to marry the cherry blossom princess, and since then, human lives have been short and fleeting. Shrines to Sakuya-Hime on Mount Fuji are said to keep the mountain from erupting.

The cherry blossom is referred to in poetry, films, and Buddhist writings. A favorite of mine, *Mono no aware*, means "Everything is transient and ephemeral."

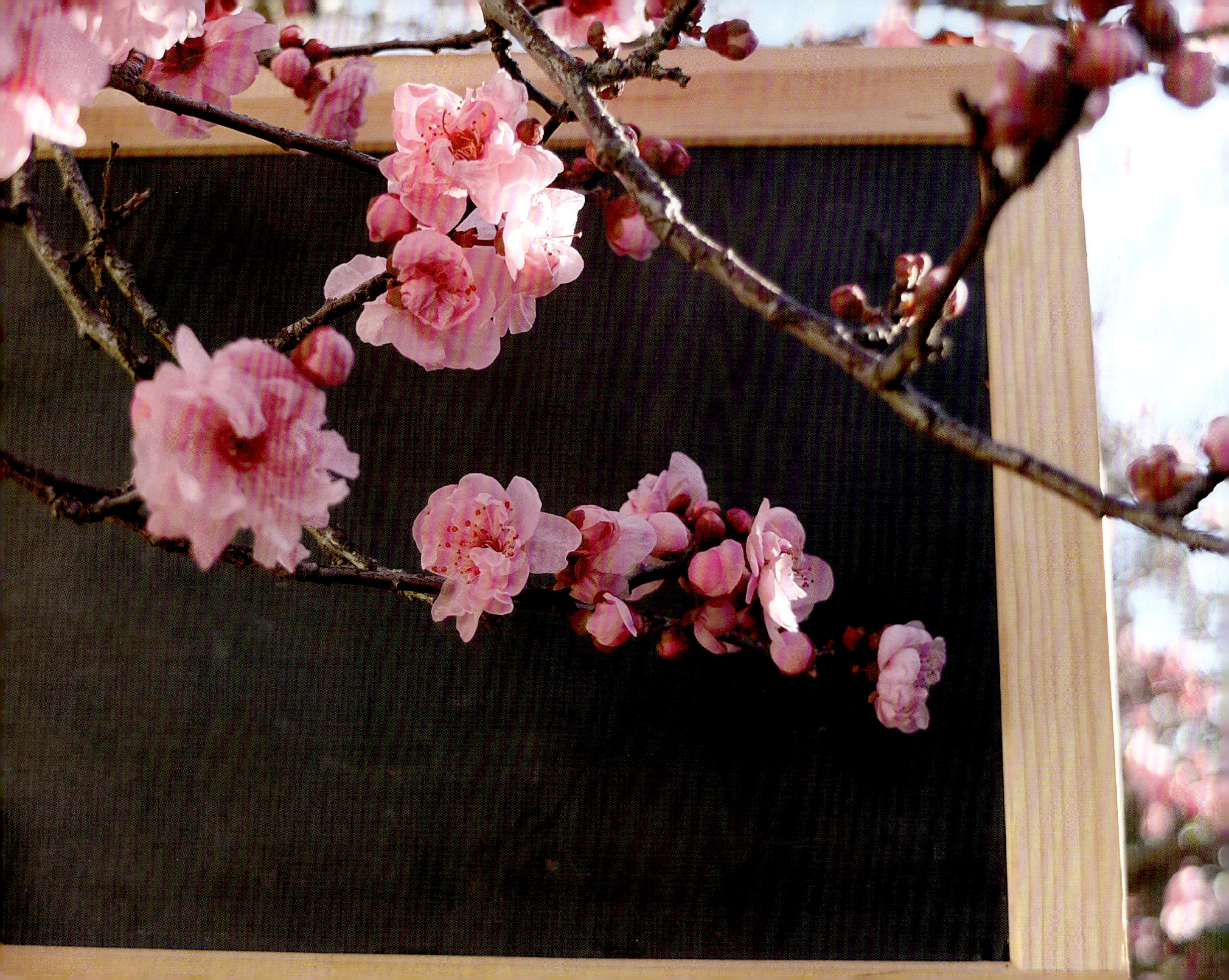

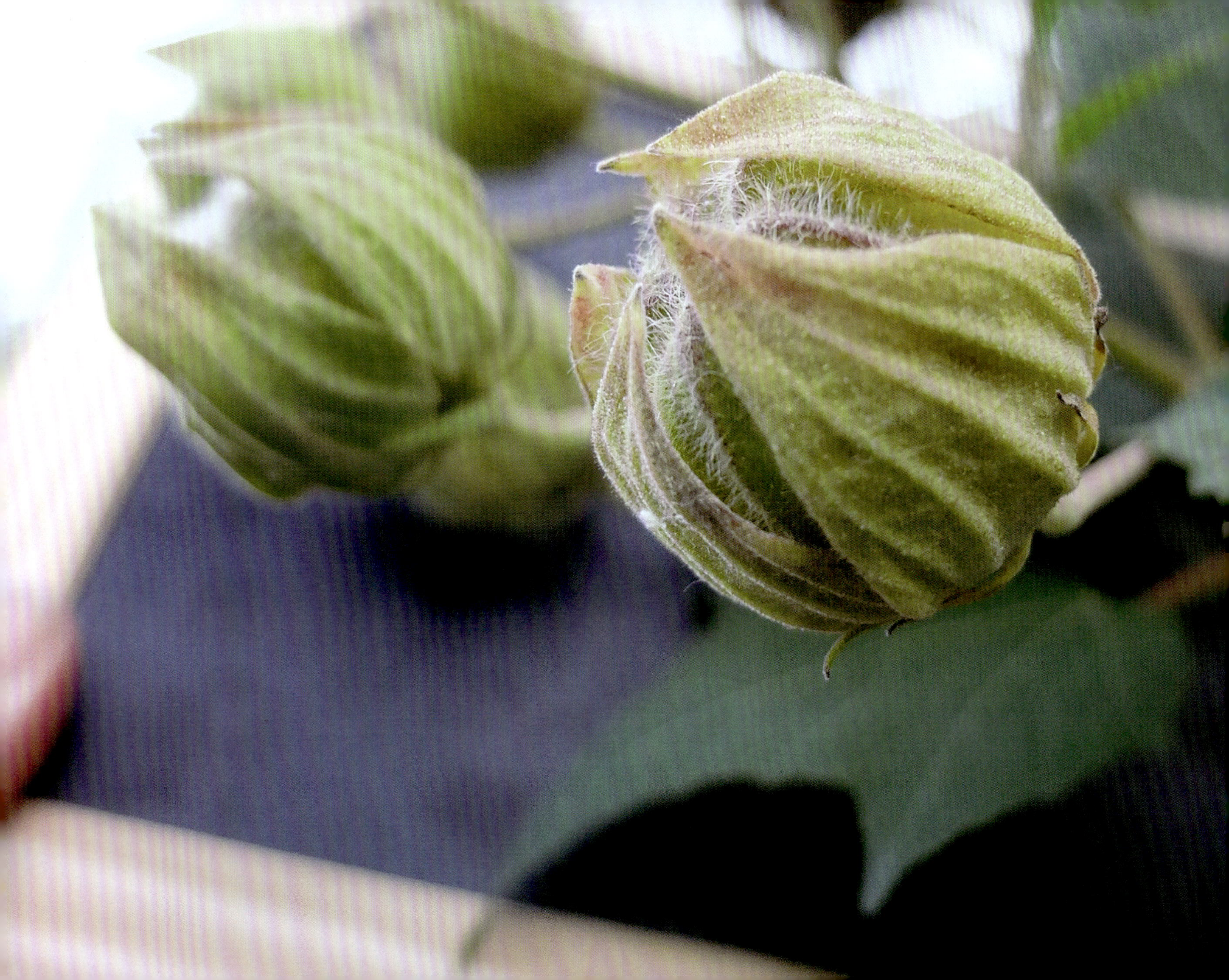

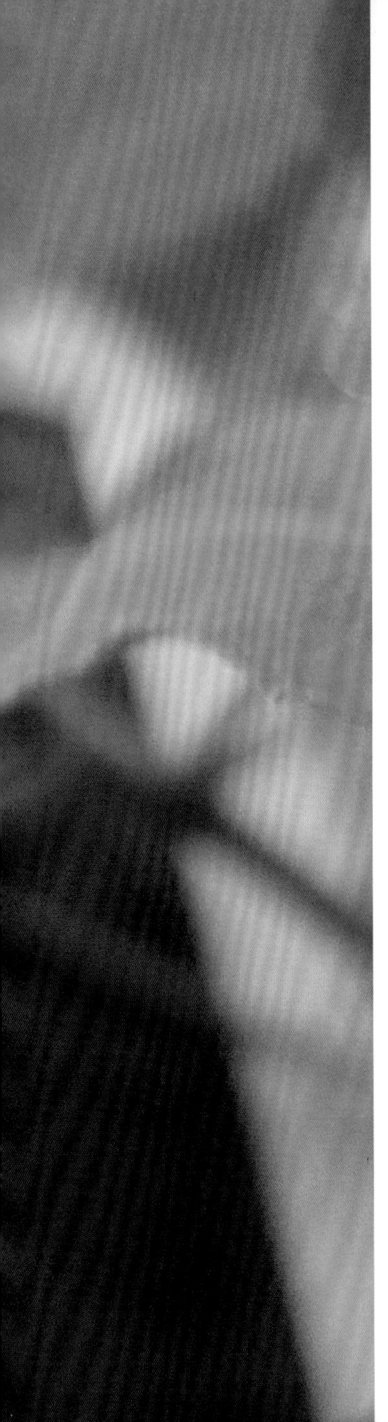

HIBISCUS

HANA KOTOBA : Gentle
JAPANESE : *Haibisukasu*
GROWING CONDITIONS : Full sun, good drainage.

At Tenryū-ji, where I discovered these early blooms, I thought of Dogen's poem:

By the spring wind
My words are blown and scattered
People may see them
The song of flowers

Dogen alludes to the same windswept movement I felt watching hibiscus seeds whirl into the air. There is a name for this seed flight in Japanese: *fubaika*.

The hibiscus in Japan is associated with gentleness despite its big, ornamental blooms; and in India, the flower is a favorite of Ganesh, the elephant-headed Hindu god of new beginnings.

These buds are about to open into brilliant flowers whose petals make one of my favorite teas.

SPIREA

HANA KOTOBA : Victory
JAPANESE : *Yukitanagi*
GROWING CONDITIONS : Sun or light shade, any soil.

The pure and audacious white of the spirea blossoms shines out of the dark green foliage as if they were stars in the night. This cultivar, appropriately called Mt. Fuji, also brings to mind the color of the snowcap that is present almost year round on the venerable mountain. Its name means "snow-covered willow."

At lunch in Kyoto, my chopsticks were wrapped in a single spirea branch, bringing the garden to my table.

I think Dogen would have been drawn to the arching shape of its branches.

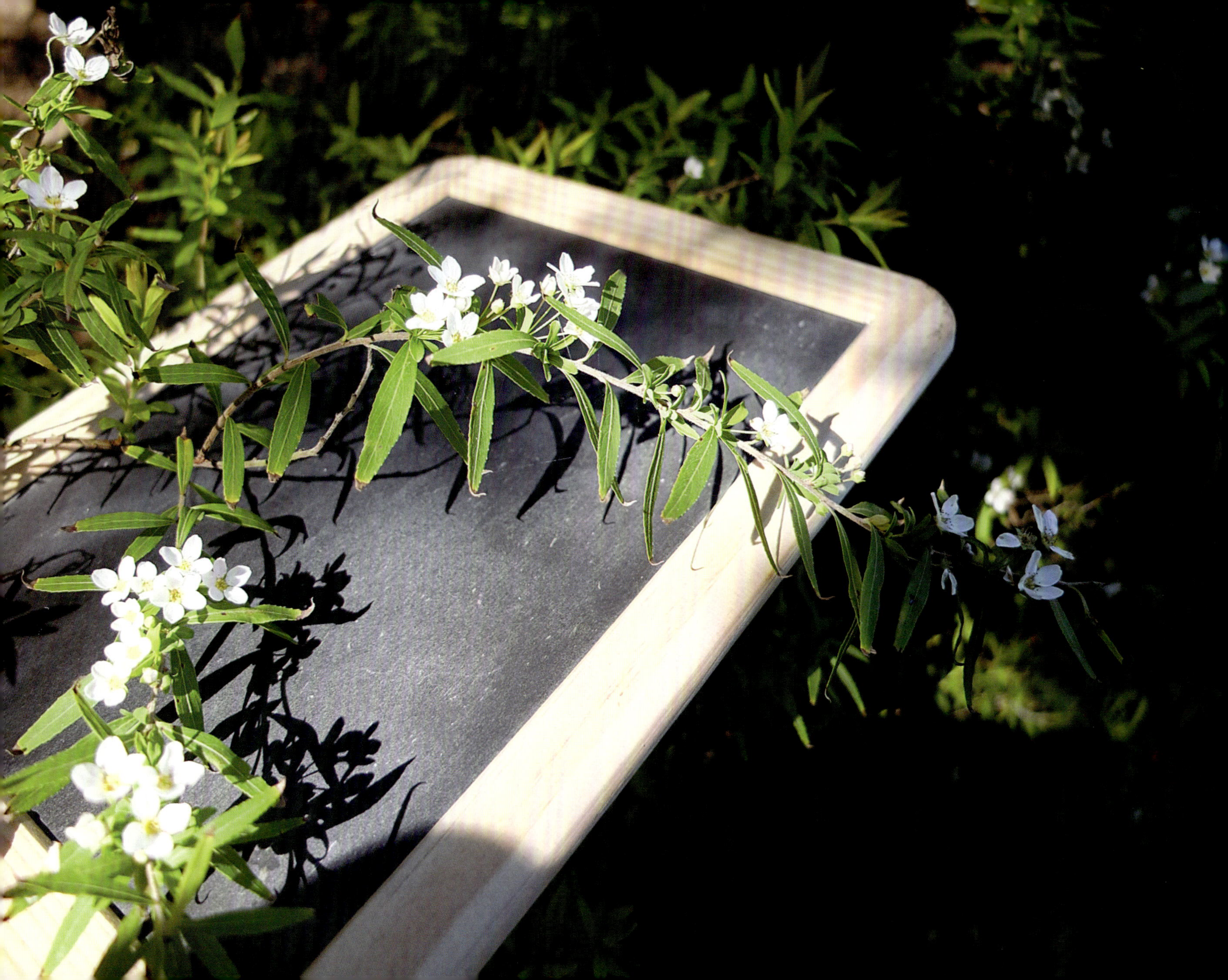

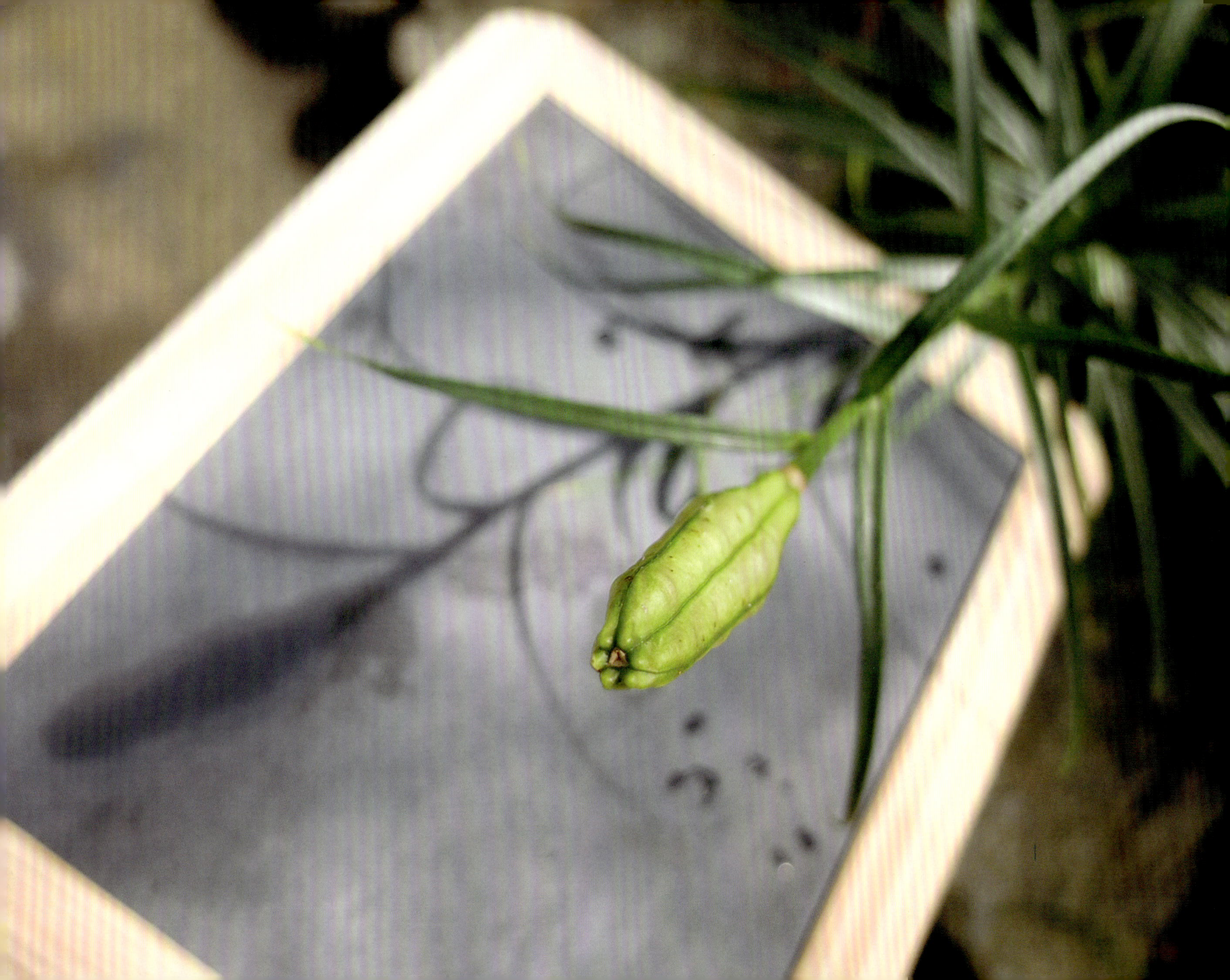

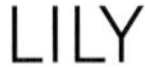

LILY

HANA KOTOBA : Orange lily—hatred and revenge. White lily—purity, chastity, and lost memory

JAPANESE : *Sayuri, shirayuri, higanbana*

GROWING CONDITIONS : Deep loose soil, moisture year round, coolness and shade at roots.

Kennin-ji had minimal color in the garden today, yet the lilies brightened my experience.

Inside each lily capsule or pod lies the hidden color of the bloom. For me, this is always surprising, like receiving a gift and not knowing what you've got until you open it. The color can be a furious orange or a heavenly, sublime white. Either way, they are unexpected guests and delights of nature.

Cultivated longer than any other ornamental flower, the plant has been around for over 3,000 years. More than 15 percent of species of lilies are indigenous to Japan. All lilies here—no matter the color—are thought of as sacred.

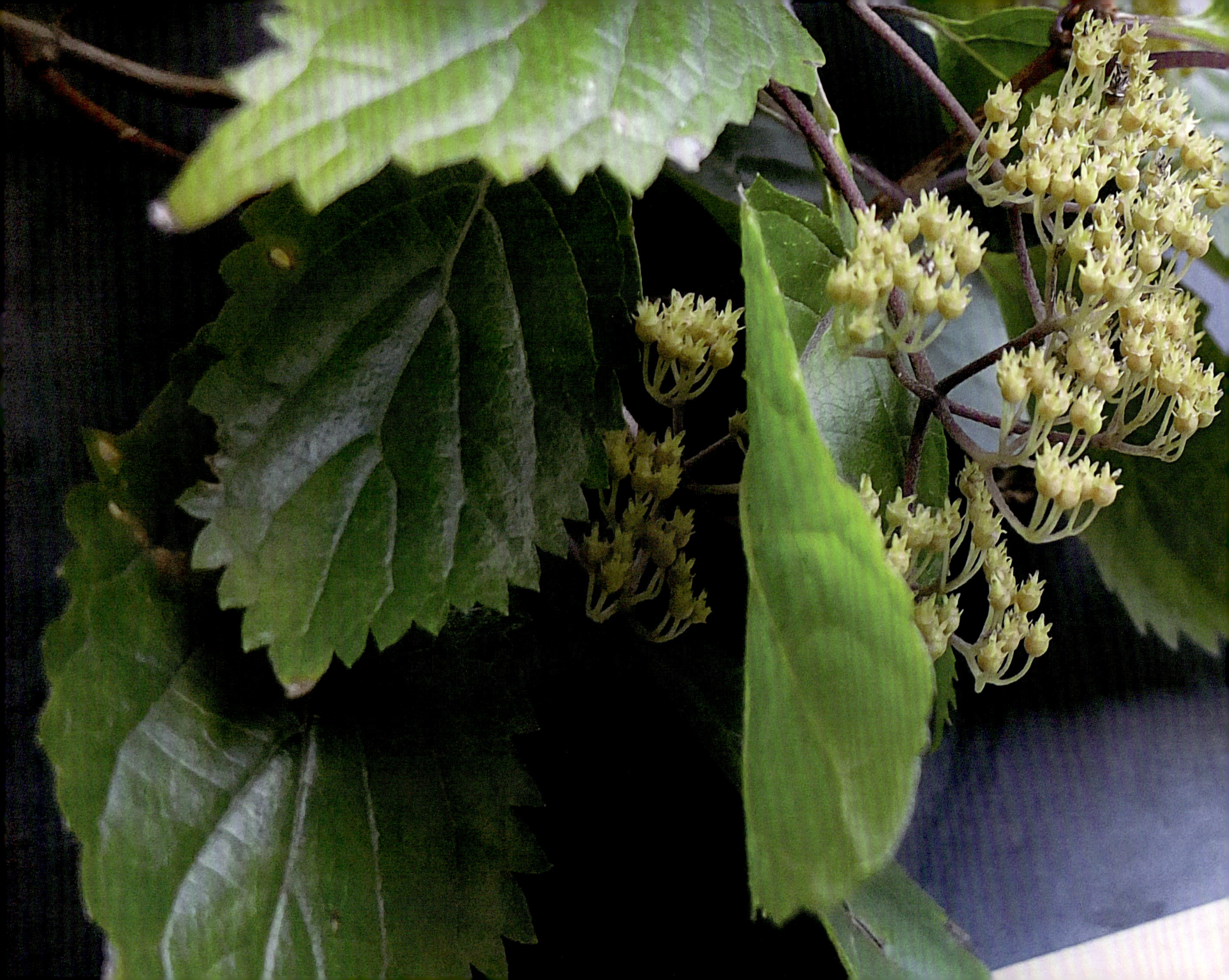

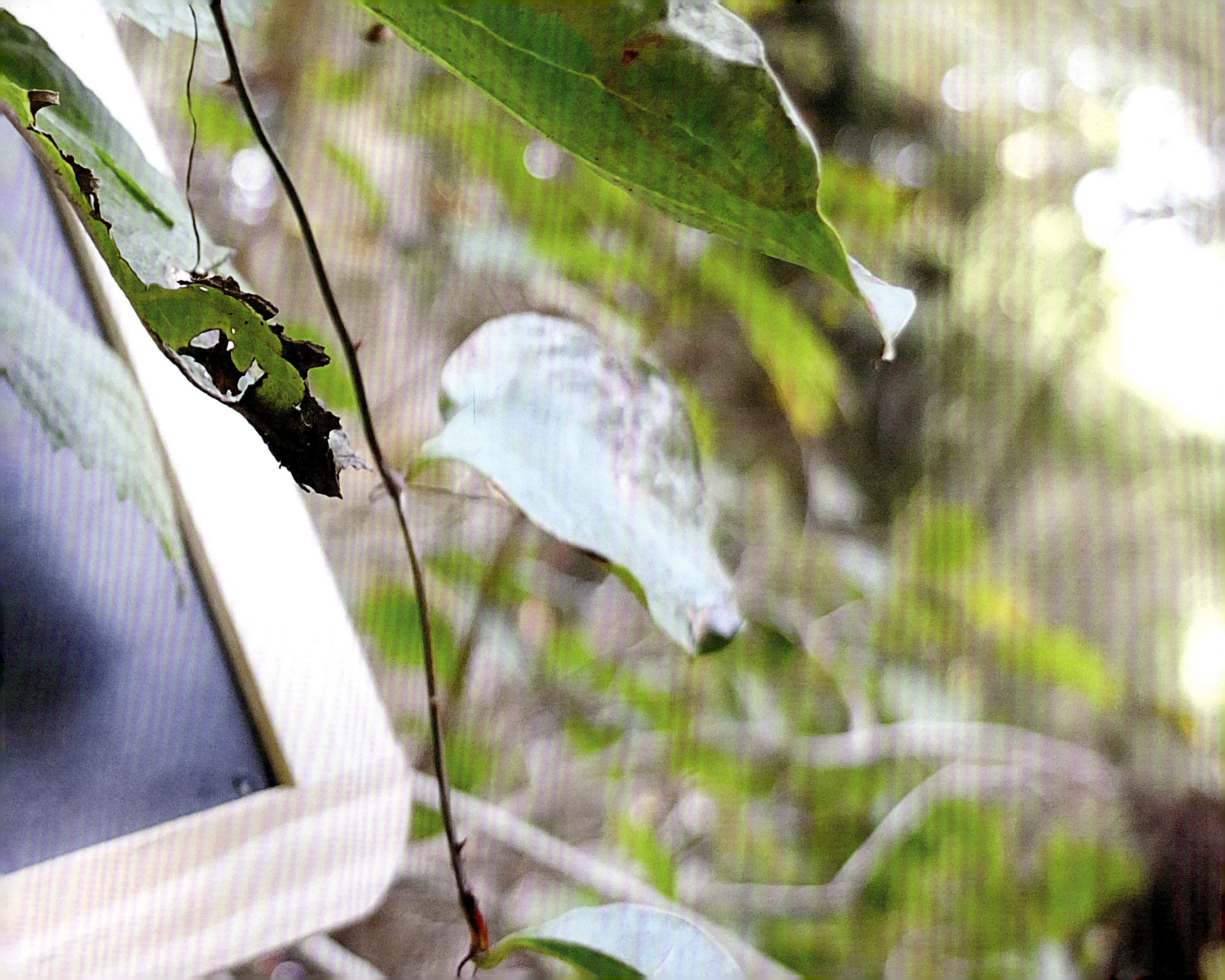

JAPANESE PLUM

HANA KOTOBA : Elegance, loyalty, devotion, harbinger of spring
JAPANESE : *Ume*
GROWING CONDITIONS : Grows in any soil; fertilize heavily. Can live at 10,000-foot elevation.

Only once have I seen a plum blossom in the midst of winter snow. I'd been told about this astonishing bloom the day before I saw it; I then trekked up the mountain behind Rinso-in. The Japanese plum stood alone, and its sole progeny, the flower, was breathtaking. Though it was too cold to smell the fragrance, the purity of the scene—the miraculous spring-pink blossom against the white bank—deeply moved me. This photograph is one of the few images I made with just one singular bloom on a tree. Dogen wrote in the "Baika" ("Plum Blossoms") section of *Shōbōgenzō*: "When flowers suddenly open on the old plum tree, it is exactly like what is said in the expression, 'When flowers open, the world arises.'" This is the coming of spring. In Confucianism, the plum blossom is a symbol of the principles and values of virtue.

Growing or eating plums has benefits. If a plum is planted on the northeast side of the garden, evil is held at bay because of its protective charm. Eating plums is said to stave off misfortune, and the *umeboshi*—a pickled plum—is delicious. I make tea by infusing the flowers and fruit in hot water and serve it cold in summer.

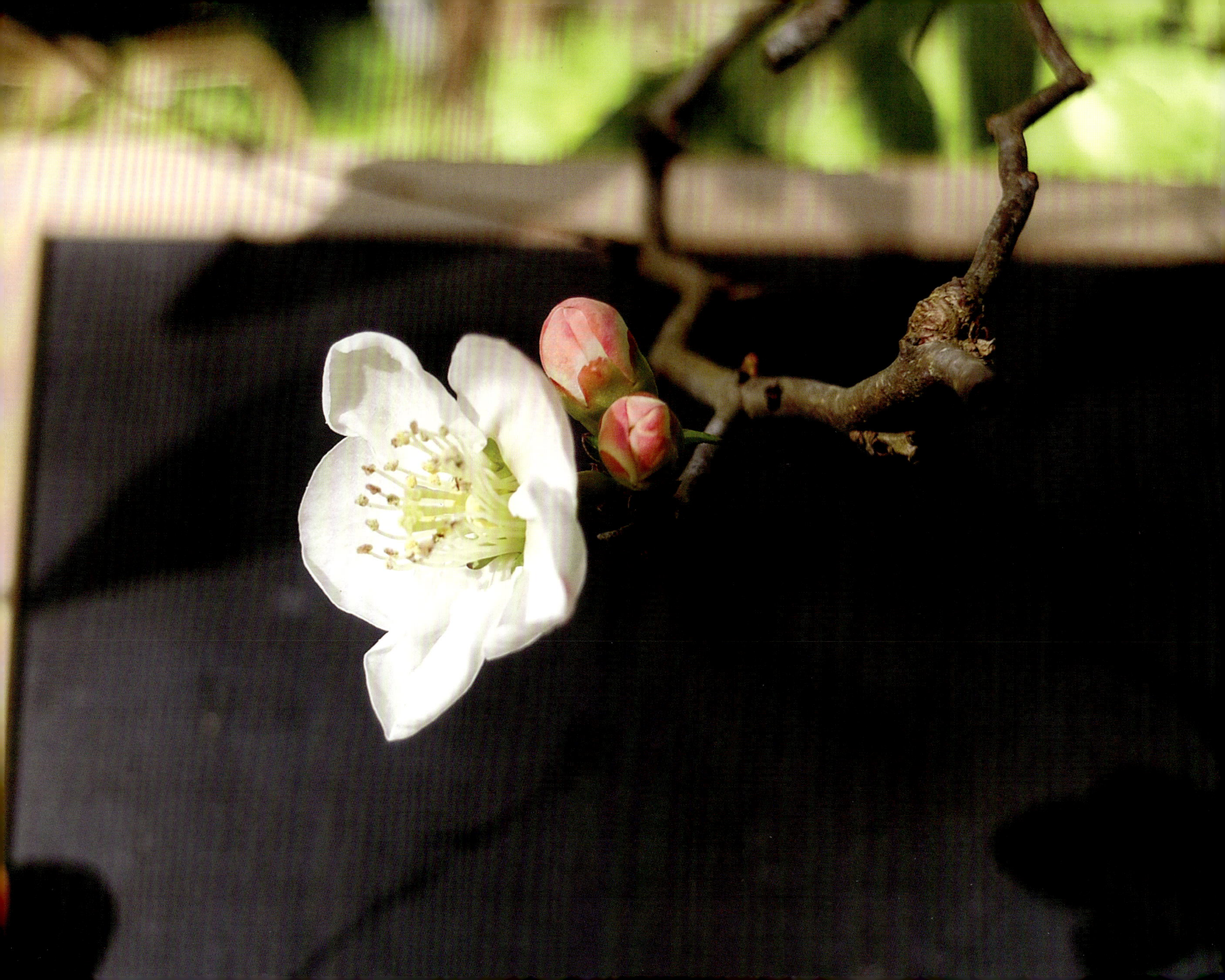

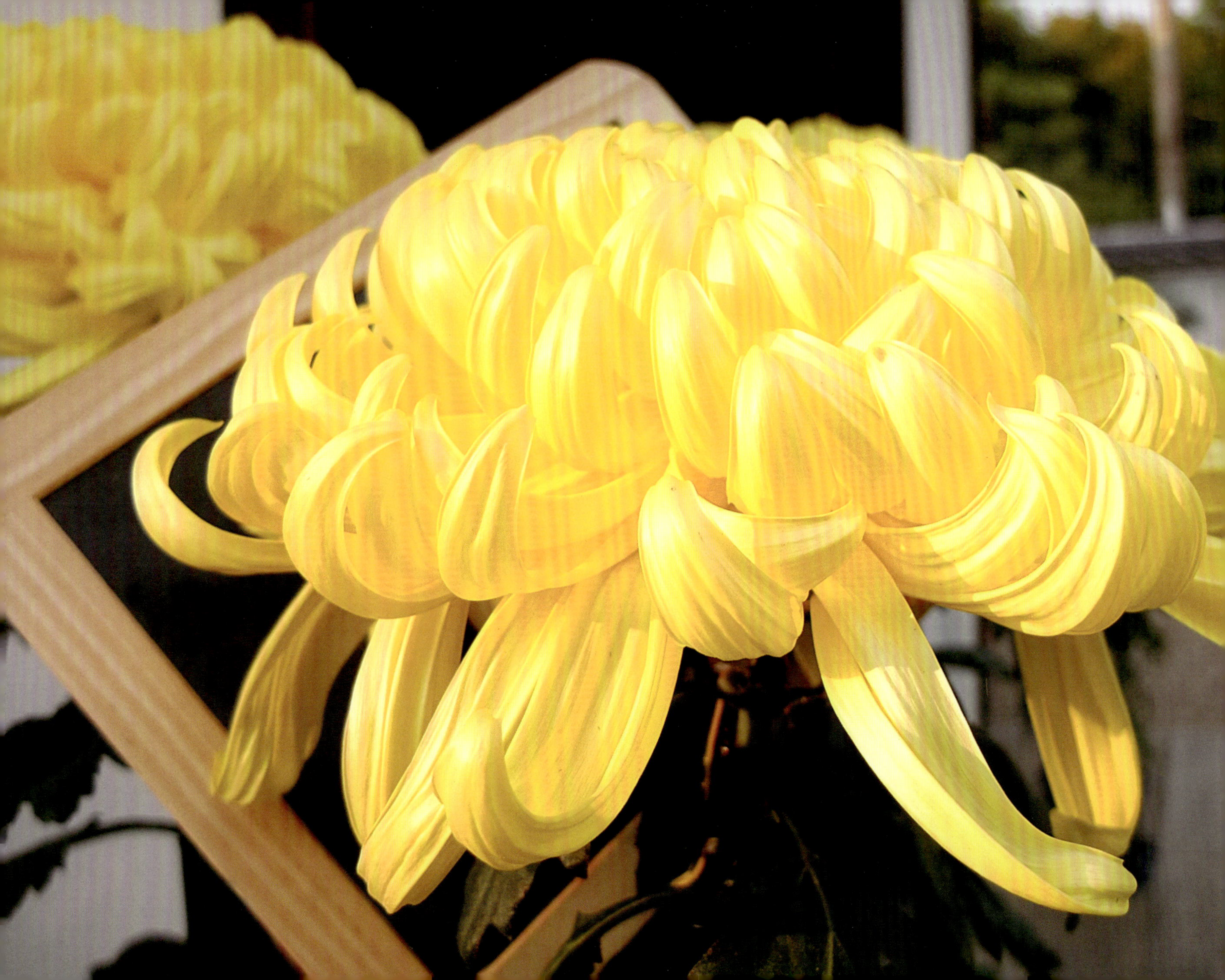

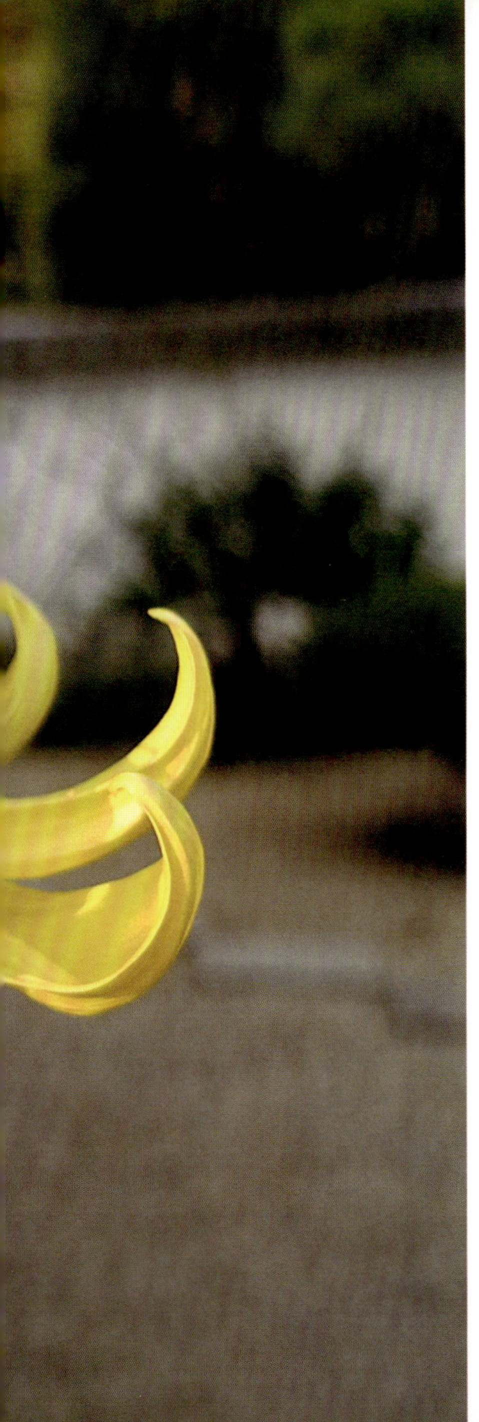

ADDENDUM

EXCERPT 1: VALLEY SOUNDS, MOUNTAIN COLORS

To hear with the ear is an everyday matter, but to hear with the eye is not always so. When you see Buddha, you see self-Buddha, other-Buddha, a large Buddha, a small Buddha. Do not be frightened by a large Buddha. Do not be put off by a small Buddha. Just see large and small Buddhas as valley sounds and mountain colors, as a broad, long tongue, and as eighty-four thousand verses. This is liberation, this is outstanding seeing.

There is a common saying that expresses this: "Totally superb, totally solid." An earlier Buddha said: "It covers heaven, it encompasses the earth." This is the purity of a spring pine, the magnificence of an autumn chrysanthemum. Just this.

Treasury of the True Dharma Eye: Zen Master Dogen's Shōbōgenzō, edited by Kaz Tanahashi (Shambhala Publications, Inc., 2010), p. 93.

COMMENTARY BY FLORENCE CAPLOW

As I write, the rain falls on the mountains outside, streaked with the last colors of autumn, and I can hear the voice of the Roaring Fork River even through the closed windows, its long, broad tongue singing teachings in my ear all day and all night, ancient sutras of the earth. The voice of the river has changed with the rain, a deeper sound than the summer river, more urgent. The river and the colors of the mountains reminds me that there is no time to waste: "Wake up, wake up!" as the wooden han (drum) at Tassajara Zen Mountain Monastery reminded me each day I was there one rainy winter long ago, its staccato call to meditation drowned by the roar of Tassajara Creek in flood. This summer when I visited Tassajara, the creek's voice was nearly silenced by drought, only a tiny, hesitant tinkling beneath the dry stones. If the whole world is Buddha, just this, then what is Tassajara Creek teaching, with its small thread of a voice? What sutra is recited by the Sierra Mountains, bedrock free of snow in the winter for the first time in five hundred years? What is the sutra of the dying aspen groves in the high mountains of Colorado? Can I bear to listen to this teaching? I hear: "Love us, love this earth from which you came and to which you return, which you have never left. This is Buddha, this is awakening. To cherish the earth fiercely is practice-realization: each pine, each aspen, each chrysanthemum most beautiful before the frost. Let your heart open and be broken. This is liberation."

EXCERPT 2: CONTINUOUS PRACTICE, PART ONE

Once you have clarity, do not neglect a single day. Wholeheartedly practice for the sake of the way and speak for the sake of the way. We know that Buddha ancestors of old did not neglect each day's endeavor. Reflect on this every day. Sit near a bright window and reflect on this, on mellow and flower-filled days. Sit in a plain building and remember it on a solitary rainy evening. Why do the moments of time steal your endeavor?

Treasury of the True Dharma Eye: Zen Master Dogen's Shōbōgenzō, edited by Kaz Tanahashi (Shambhala Publications, Inc., 2010), p. 348.

COMMENTARY BY MICHAEL WENGER

Dogen's garden is right before us. His clarity here is not the clarity of subtraction but the clarity of connection. To practice in the midst of connectedness is wondrousness. Buddhism is a living entity alive in our tender participation with everything. Neglect encourages weeds. Weeds in themselves can be used to nourish, but they too need to be cultivated, to be practiced with. By manifesting ourselves, the world comes alive. Time can momentarily steal our sense of aliveness if we lose the sense of continuity and participation. Each flowering is a culmination, an ending and a new beginning. Dogen may have lived a long time ago, but his connection to us is palpable. His teachings, his garden, lives on through us. Don't waste time!

EXCERPT 3: EIGHT VERSES GIVEN TO A ZEN PERSON

Clouds disappearing in the blue sky, a crane's mind at ease;
Waves constant on the ancient shore, a fish swims slowly.
Who can focus their eyes on this vague edge?
From the hundred-foot pole, take another step.

Dogen's Extensive Record: A Translation of the Eihei Koroku, Vol. 10, translated by Taigen Dan Leighton and Shohaku Okumura, edited and introduced by Taigen Dan Leighton (Wisdom Publications, 2010), p. 624

COMMENTARY BY SHINSHU ROBERTS

This old mind of delusion finally clarified. In its nest high up in the jewel forest a crane sighs. The waves continue endlessly to bring the moon's reflection on its ancient shore. Who swims their way into the dragon's gate? Who can see the reflection's bright way? The edge is not vague when we step into its boundary. Knee deep in muddy water, stepping off the 100-foot pole, it's just this moment. Did you notice? Like fish leaping clear of the one and many. Splash! A crane stretching its wings flying in the endless sky. A cold nest in the forest pine.

EXCERPT 4: GENJŌKŌAN (10)

Within the dusty world and beyond, there are innumerable aspects and characteristics; we only see or grasp as far as the power of our eye of study and practice can see. When we listen to the reality of myriad things, we must know that there are inexhaustible characteristics in both ocean and mountains, and there are many other worlds in the four directions. This is true not only in the external world, but also right under our feet or within a single drop of water.

Realizing Genjōkōan: The Key to Dogen's Shōbōgenzō, by Shohaku Okumura (Wisdom Publications, 2010), p. 3.

COMMENTARY BY SHOHAKU OKUMURA

"The dusty world" refers to the ordinary secular world, where we view and judge with our discriminating mind using the yardstick from the human point of view. "The world beyond" refers to the world of the Buddha-dharma, that is beyond the standard of human sentiments based on emptiness, interconnectedness, oneness, and equality of all things. Dogen is saying that we need to see both ways at the same time. In order to see and hear the reality of all things, we need to be free from our karmic view. Still we see, study clearly each and everything we encounter using both discriminative and beyond-discriminative wisdom. He loved plum blossoms. At Eiheiji, plum blossoms bloom in the early spring while the world is still completely covered with snow. He gave a dharma discourse on the fifteenth day of the first month in 1247. At the end of the discourse he offered a Chinese poem:

The family style is pure white, like plum blossoms, snow, and the moon. At the time of flowering, fortunately there is a way to protect the body. The clouds are bright, the water is delightful, and our effort is totally perfect. Without sensing it, our entire body enters the emperor's capitol.

In this poem, "a way to protect the body" refers to zazen practice. The clouds and the waters refer to the clouds-and-water monks, the practitioners at Eiheiji. The emperor's capitol refers to Changan (Choan), which means eternal peace (nirvana). Dogen saw the concrete things such as plum blossoms, snow, and the monks sitting in the monks' hall, here and now. And also, he saw eternal peace right in practice of zazen.

EXCERPT 5: JUKO-STYLE POEMS

The bright green color of the peach and plum trees so shiny and
lustrous,
Manifesting in these very branches the same spring of hundreds
of generations;
It is foolish to despise what is close by or to value something that
Is far away;
Right now remove all doubts by seeing what you see and hearing
What you hear.

The Zen Poetry of Dogen: Verses from the Mountain of Eternal Peace, translated by Steven Heine (Tuttle Publishing, 1997), p. 142.44-C

COMMENTARY BY REB ANDERSON

Is this green color the visible one that appears in our mind as though it were not itself mind, but external to it? Or is Dogen speaking of a fresher green . . . long before these shiny green ghosts were born together with a self?

We may know that the images of peach and plum trees are like skeletons of the authentic peach and plum. It would be sad and silly to despise them, shrink back from them, and then reach out for the fresh peaches of our authentic life.

In such a mind field of lustrous trees of illusion, what is an appropriate response? Dogen suggests this *"seeing what you see . . ."* is neither to esteem nor despise these colorful trees; it is rather to become intimate with them. This may be the appropriate foolishness which Buddha ancestors encourage and embody for all of us.

ABOUT MARCIA LIEBERMAN

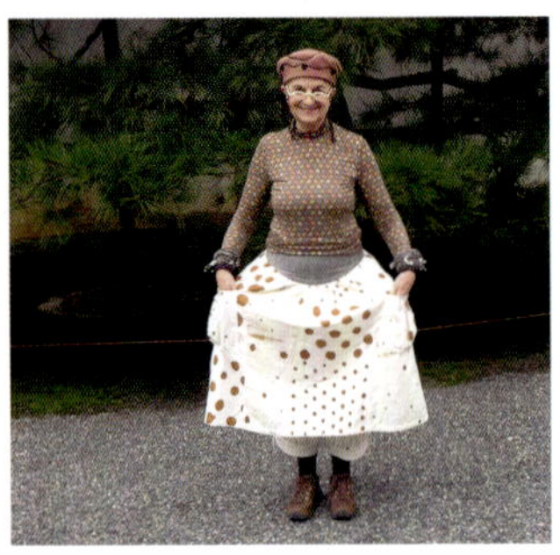

Marcia Lieberman is a photographer, author, and academic. Her work has focused on people of note and particular projects driven by an idea or subject that concerns her. Published books include *When Divas Confess*, and *Being Still*.

During her years of teaching at the University of California, Berkeley, and California College of Art, Oakland, Lieberman lectured on time and space, dwellings, representation of time passing, and the interview as a visual entity. She resides in San Francisco and passes much of her time at the San Francisco Zen Center, where being still is a daily practice. Her interest in temple arts has led her to study the way of tea and altar flower arranging. She recently finished her graduate courses in Buddhist Scholarship at the Institute of Buddhist Studies, Graduate Theological Seminary, University of California, Berkeley.

ABOUT TAIGEN DAN LEIGHTON

Taigen Dan Leighton, a dharma heir and priest in the Suzuki Roshi lineage, leads the Ancient Dragon Zen Gate in Chicago. He is the author of several books, including *Zen Questions: Zazen, Dogen, and the Spirit of Creative Inquiry; Visions of Awakening Space and Time: Dogen and the Lotus Sutra; Faces of Compassion: Classic Bodhisattva Archetypes and Their Modern Expression;* and *Just This Is It: Dongshan and the Practice of Suchness;* and has translated a number of Zen texts, including *Dogen's Extensive Record, Dogen's Pure Standards for the Zen Community,* and *Cultivating the Empty Field.* Leighton teaches online at the Berkeley Graduate Theological Union, from where he has a PhD.

ACKNOWLEDGMENTS

Making a book like this includes folks that inspired, encouraged, supported, and insisted. In particular I'd like to thank the late Abbot Steve Stuckey for his early insightful comment to use my gardening knowledge in studying Dogen; Taigen Leighton for his regular meetings, editorial comments, and beautiful introduction to the book; Marc Treib for meeting me in Kyoto and Berkeley to discuss this project; Brandy Kuhl, library director at Helen Crocker Russell Library of Horticulture, for poring through heavy texts and resource material to find the right bloom; Birgit Wick, the book designer, who shaped my materials so that they could speak with such creative style; the five Dogen scholars who generously responded to my inquiry and added the important commentaries; Elizabeth Orr for an impeccable editorial hand in my writings; Elissa Rabellino for making mistakes disappear.

In the field, two devoted graduate students from Kyoto University translated and helped me navigate in temple gardens: Cherry Haishishen and Oyake Yui.

A grateful bow to Gordon Goff and his continued support of my work.

For the many everyday acts of kindness and encouragement to stay the course in this long process, I especially note Linda Ruth Cutts, Jane Wattenberg, Patty McManus, Joanne Rollins, and my beloved family.

These persons, and more unnamed, keep fragrance in my everyday life.

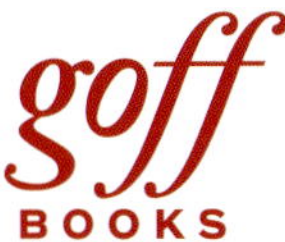

Published by Goff Books, an Imprint of ORO Editions.
Executive publisher: Gordon Goff.
www.goffbooks.com
info@goffbooks.com

Graphic Design: Birgit Wick, wickdesignstudio.com
Text and Images: Marcia Lieberman; author photo by Noah Lieberman.
Font: Avenir
Goff Books Project Coordinator: Kirby Anderson
10 9 8 7 6 5 4 3 2 1 First Edition

Library of Congress data available upon request. World Rights: available.
ISBN: 978-1-951541-08-8
Color separations and printing: ORO Group Ltd.
Printed in China.
International distribution: www.goffbooks.com/distribution

ORO Editions makes a continuous effort to minimize the overall carbon footprint of its publications. As part of this goal, ORO Editions, in association with Global ReLeaf, arranges to plant trees to replace those used in the manufacturing of the paper produced for its books. Global ReLeaf is an international campaign run by American Forests, one of the world's oldest nonprofit conservation organizations. Global ReLeaf is American Forests' education and action program that helps individuals, organizations, agencies, and corporations improve the local and global environment by planting and caring for trees.